CISTERCIAN STUDIES SERIES: NUMBER FOURTEEN

THE ABBOT IN MONASTIC TRADITION

CISTERCIAN STUDIES SERIES

CISTERCIAN STUDIES SERIES: NUMBER FOURTEEN

THE ABBOT
IN MONASTIC TRADITION

*A contribution to the history of the perpetual character
of the office of religious superiors in the West*

Dom Pierre Salmon OSB

translated by
Claire Lavoie

CISTERCIAN PUBLICATIONS
CONSORTIUM PRESS
Washington, D.C.
1972

This book was first published by Sirey, Paris, in the collection, Histoire et Sociologie de l'Eglise, under the title, *L'abbé dans la tradition monastique*.

Copyright 1962 by Dom Pierre Salmon–Editions Sirey, 22 Rue Soufflot, Paris 5ᵉ France.

© Copyright, Cistercian Publications, Inc., 1972.
Spencer, Massachusetts 01562

Library of Congress Catalog Card Number: 78–158955
Cistercian Studies Series ISBN 0–87907–800–6
This Volume ISBN 0–87907–814–6

Printed in the Republic of Ireland by
Cahill & Co. Limited, Parkgate Printing Works, Dublin

CONTENTS

PREFACE

IN OUR CONTEMPORARY WORLD, as secular and infatuated with technology as it is, monasteries still occupy an important place. It can even be said that, since the middle of the nineteenth century, they have experienced a veritable renaissance. Hundreds of houses built in all corners of the earth shelter tens of thousands of religious who constitute a growing force within the Church and within our Age.[1] This force has been active for more than fifteen centuries. It has exercised its influence from the most ancient times, throughout the Middle Ages, and after the Council of Trent.[2]

In each monastery authority rests primarily with the superior. He is responsible for the internal government and external activity. He watches over the observance of the Rule and assures the outward influence of a "city" which is never entirely cloistered. His election and his status have a significance which historians bring to light but which the general public does not fully grasp. In order to inform the latter and justify the former, Dom Salmon retraces the peculiar vicissitudes of the abbatial charge.

1. The official catalogue, *SS. Patriarchae Benedicti familiae confederatae,* at the present time numbers 12,131 confederated Benedictines, to whom must be added the Cistercians, Trappists, Camaldolese, Vallombrosans, Silvestrines, and many others who are not as strictly attached to the Rule of Saint Benedict.

2. A description of this activity will be found in all history books. Numerous scientific studies, such as the conferences of the sixth week of Spoleto (1959) and the Martinian celebrations (1961), have more accurately revealed the role of monks in the history of civilization.

Should this office be perpetual or temporary? Its essential nature gives an answer which events at times deny. By the ultimate identification of the primitive functions of guide and superior the abbot is marked out as a *Father*.[3] Among Saint Benedict's disciples, it is actually no longer a question of distinguishing between the spiritual director and the *higoumene,* as it was among the desert ascetics: the monastery is the home of a family, governed by a father who is elected but, like all fathers, is endowed with an authority which only death, as a rule, can terminate.

As a matter of fact, the Benedictine Rule merely implies this perpetuity, but Emperor Justinian and Gregory the Great confirm it.[4] Benedict of Aniane and Cluny agree with this. A change takes place only *defuncto abbate* and the community usually chooses the successor.[5]

However, there were various obstacles which thwarted the application of the practice. First of all there was the self-interest and caprice of the princes who, as early as the Frankish era, arbitrarily disposed of the abbatial charge;[6] then during the Classical Age, there were the institution of general chapters,[7] the example of magistracies,[8] and the struggle waged against the commendam.[9]

The authority of the general chapters exposed the abbots to dismissal. This form was adopted notably by the Carthusians, the

3. In the East, the two functions were originally distinct: that of the spiritual father was permanent.

4. The texts leave no other doubt except with regard to the dependence of the latter on the former.

5. Some African Councils and Popes such as Pelagius have laid down this principle of election. Nevertheless, it happened that some abbots chose their own successor during the barbarian era. At Cluny, the general, as a rule, appointed all the abbots and priors at will. Finally, the Holy See itself has often intervened since the eleventh century.

6. The Frankish kings, in particular, often treated the monasteries as their own property on the pretext of their ancestors' generosity or of simple patronage.

7. This institution born in the twelfth century tended to place the superior general under the power of the periodical assembly of the local superiors.

8. It is known that these magistracies were conferred for a brief period.

9. The perpetuity of the commendators was a threat to the point of ruin.

Premonstratensians, and also the Minors.[10] It is possible that the example of the Italian cities inspired Tolomei to adopt the rule of annual elections for the Olivetan Congregation which he founded.[11] The Hermits of Saint Augustine had already limited the term of the prior general to three years (1255), and the Celestines were the first among the monks to observe a similar restriction (1259). The abuse of the commendam induced Louis Barbo, in his Congregation of Saint Justine (later known as the Cassinese Congregation), to make of the abbot a mere delegate to the general chapter which meets every year.[12] The same reasons were invoked by the Congregation of Valladolid. Hereafter, the principle of perpetuity is nearly everywhere abandoned.[13] The Society of Jesus adhered to it, but the wind remained contrary. When Dom Gueranger wanted to restore the primitive principle, the Holy See hesitated, demanding several three year terms of probation.[14] Then a resounding conversion: the Congregation of Saint Justine declared itself in favor of perpetuity. Today almost all Benedictines have perpetual abbots, whereas other orders prefer a periodical renewal.[15]

Contemporary scholars have calculated the arguments for and against perpetuity. We have raised the main point, which is conformity to the natural order: spiritual fatherhood. Dom Butler insists on lasting responsibility, Dom Molitor on the in-

10. Innocent II provided for the deposition of Premonstratensian superiors who would deviate from the statutes of the Order (1131). The general chapter of the Carthusians in 1140 reserves deposition to itself, and several new orders also left the general chapter to determine the duration of the superior's charge. Many were the vicissitudes among the Minors. The Preachers and Carmelites originally had perpetual superiors general.

11. Tolomei had been military gonfalonier and captain of the people.

12. The precariousness of the charge could not be pushed much further.

13. Little by little, nearly all the orders give it up. However, Bursfeld maintained perpetuity.

14. Rome granted perpetuity only after three, then four successive three year terms. Dom Gueranger's successor was declared perpetual (1877).

15. Actually, it was mainly political circumstances which imposed perpetuity on Saint Justine. The majority of religious superiors today are elected or appointed for a determined length of time, fixed by Canon Law or the constitutions of each institute.

convenience of lodging several successive abbots under the same roof and the turmoil of frequent elections.

The dangers are unquestionable: physical or administrative incompetence can make of the abbot a formidable hindrance to the moral and material interests of the monastery, an irregularity which was often repeated during the Middle Ages and even up to modern times. A radical cure presents itself: deposition, if the abbot has not the wisdom to resign.[16]

It was the duty of the Holy See or the general chapter to pronounce the deposition.[17] And resignations were so numerous that the practice had to be checked.[18] By these measures, as well as by a fixed term of office, the danger of an unfortunate government was avoided.

This history, handled with the precision characteristic of all Dom Salmon's works,[19] throws a vivid light on the monastic past and constitutes a scientific defence[20] of the principle of perpetuity.

16. The visitation was the occasion for examining the government of the abbot. A list of causes for deposition was set out in Cistercian legislation.

17. In the High Middle Ages the bishops often deposed and the councils regulated their interventions. The papacy acted more and more often during the Classical Age and, by this means and by its reserves, assumed the right of frequent selection, allowing for long periods of vacancy in order to collect revenues.

18. Numerous from the beginning, these were very numerous in the thirteenth and fourteenth centuries, due to incompetence or the threat of insolvency, or as a result of pressure; there was also the need for solitude and the desire of a comfortable retirement. It was necessary to curb this practice by demanding a just cause.

19. Dom Salmon, born in Goncourt (Hte. Marne), entered the Benedictine monastery of Clervaux in 1920. He was appointed abbot of Saint Jerome in Rome in 1935 by Pius XI and charged with the task of the revision of the Vulgate, succeeding Dom Quentin. Under his direction, there have been published to date nine volumes of the Vulgate (the tenth volume is at press) and seven volumes of *Collectanea Biblica Latina*. He has also published: *Le Lectionnaire de Luxeuil*, I, *Edition et étude comparative*, Rome, 1944; II, *Etude paléographique et liturgique*, ib. 1953; *Etude sur les insignes du Pontife dans le rit romain*, Rome, 1955; *L'Office divin*, Paris, 1959; *Les Tituli Psalmorum des manuscrits latins*, Paris-Rome, 1959; *L'Eglise en prière, Introduction à la Liturgie*, chapter on "La prière des heures," Paris, 1961.

20. The author exposes the facts with a perfect impartiality, concealing none of the miseries of ecclesiastical and monastic government, and seeking with great insight all the causes behind the options.

We had at first interpreted the author's thought with some reserve, considering the drawbacks of the perpetuity of the Episcopal See. The difference was quickly manifest, and we believe, with the learned Abbot of Saint Jerome, that "it is not the perpetuity of the superior which is harmful, but the absence of a control and appropriate means of remedying the inconveniences which spring from weaknesses, abuses, and incompetence."

G. Le Bras

INTRODUCTION

THE GREAT MAJORITY of religious superiors today are elected or appointed for a determined length of time, fixed once for all by Canon Law or the Constitutions of each institute; under the present law, even their re-eligibility is limited to a certain number of times. The most common regime is that of temporary superiors. It was not always so. In the beginning and for long centuries afterwards, all religious superiors were in office for life. Witnesses to this ancient tradition continue to exist: monastic orders still have perpetual abbots.* How and why has the primitive institution given way to the more usual practice of modern days? Has the institution of lifetime abbots remained intact in all respects; has it not encountered grave difficulties, has it not been abandoned for long periods and in areas where the monastic life has been most fervent and prosperous? Is not the lifetime regime of superiors a primitive and obsolete mode of religious government whose normal evolution would tend towards a system of periodical replacement, which would allow for an easy and quick resolution of fatal crises of authority or instances of personal incompetence?

The following pages attempt to answer these questions by retracing the history of the lifetime abbatial charge. In order to establish certain limitations, and because religious life has developed

---

*Since the French publication of this book in 1962, various Benedictine Congregations and also the Cistercians of the Strict Observance have modified this practice: abbots are now elected for an indefinite period of time. (Tr.)

differently in the East and the West, this study will be confined to
the evolution of the regime of superiors in the Latin Church.
However, monastic life derives its origins from the East and, as a
result, that is where the history of religious superiors begins; from
this source we have gathered the facts and texts which can explain
or justify the western practice up until the moment when it was
fully established and had its own proper organization.

To see how the notion of temporary superiors, and even temporary abbots, has been reached, we must investigate the regime of
superiors as it appeared in the first orders instituted from the twelfth
century. Abandoning the traditional monastic form, these orders
no longer had abbots: would they also immediately renounce the
perpetuity of superiors? Once they did arrive at this, is it their
example which encouraged the monks themselves to renounce the
principle of lifetime abbots? Such are the questions which lead to
an investigation of the regime of superiors, among the Canons
Regular, the Carthusians, the Mendicants, etc. We must then
uncover the causes which led certain monks, the Celestines and the
Olivetans, to have the first temporary abbots: were they inspired
by the new orders or were they subject to other influences? The
new orders are not here considered as though they were the very
flowering of the monastic order; they are referred to only as
witnesses to a stage in the development of the organization of
religious life, at the moment when there is proven to be a certain
faltering in the institution of the lifetime regime. Their confronta-
tion with monastic observances on the point in question permits us,
on the one hand, to place the problem of the duration of the abbatial
charge within the context of the history of religious institutions
and, on the other, to establish more accurately the determining
element of the lifetime regime.

The important thing is to distinguish between what is inherent in
the monastic institution and what is due to the influence of
similar institutions and historical circumstances. The political
monasticism of the Middle Ages or the influence of Italian communes and republics from the eleventh to the fifteenth century, the
new forms of religious life beginning from the twelfth century, the

transitory forms motivated by powerful reform movements and marked by a violent reaction against certain abuses, such as at Cluny and at Saint Justine of Padua—have all of these imprinted a deep and enduring stamp on the monastic institution; have they substantially transformed it, especially where the abbatial regime is concerned?

It will be seen that the element which determines the lifetime abbatial regime is the idea of spiritual fatherhood, which entails, as a consequence, the stability of the superior as well as that of the religious. It is in the measure that the monks in the various monasteries have correctly applied the ideal of spiritual fatherhood and sonship, according to the proper mode of each form of monastic life, that this life has attained its perfection, beyond all vicissitudes and obstacles, both external and internal.

The division of the subject is imposed by the stages of monastic history itself, since the lifetime abbot is one of the characteristic marks, one of the main elements of the monastic institution. It is by following the evolution of the latter that we can arrive at a fair idea of the regime of its superiors. The unfolding of this history will better enable us to see whether the lifetime abbatial office is always apt to respond to its aims, and whether it still remains a valid form of government—like the system of temporary superiors characteristic of modern orders and congregations—and is consistent with the monastic institution itself.

Since the aim of this work is to establish and justify the lifetime regime of abbots, we will limit ourselves to establishing facts and citing texts, deliberately leaving aside all speculative or spiritual explanation. However, more than one text cited points to the meaning and worth of the institution. It would not be difficult to develop these ideas and theoretically legitimate the system of lifetime abbots, but the particular exigencies of the method prevented dealing with this aspect of the question.

PART ONE

THE ORIGINS TO THE TENTH CENTURY

CHAPTER ONE

BEFORE THE GREAT LATIN RULES

IN THE BEGINNINGS of the religious life, before the organization of monasticism, there were no superiors: there was no need for them. Nevertheless, fervent Christians who sought to lead a more perfect life were not abandoned to their own resources, subject solely to the interventions of the ecclesiastical hierarchy. They had recourse to brothers who were more experienced, more prudent, and had a reputation for sanctity, in order to be initiated and directed by them. Each one chose for himself a guide, *senior,* of whom he first of all expected the maturity and experience which are customary in older persons. This latter was not merely a master who taught, but a pedagogue who reprimanded, corrected, and trained; he was also, and before all else, a spiritual and perfect man. He who guides his brothers, with an authority certified by long practice, must himself have realized, at least to a degree above the average, the manner of life toward which he directs the others.[1]

These different aspects are contained in the word "father," *abba, pater.* It expresses the maturity, experience and perfection which are fitting for one who engenders others into a new life and guides them through the difficulties which it presents; and since it is a matter of leading them to God, this fatherhood is a participation in the divine Fatherhood. It extends to the whole growth of

1. Cf. I. Hausherr, "La direction spirituelle en Orient autrefois," in *Orientalia Christiana Analecta,* 144. Rome, 1955, p. 55–57.

the Christian life and to spiritual training according to the spirit of filiation. But in the long series of good works which are so many steps toward the perfection of the child of God, there is one that holds a special place: entrance into monastic life. That is why the mention of spiritual fatherhood among the ancients is linked up not only with the memory of entrance into the Christian life, but also with initiation into the religious life. For them, that man is a father who sets one on the journey toward God, whether he engenders into the Christian life or leads to the perfect life.[2]

The word *abba* assumed its meaning during the flowering of Egyptian monasticism in the fourth century: it denotes first of all and principally a spiritual man, regardless of the actual direction of sons. The *abba* is essentially a man of experience, a perfect monk who has fully realized in himself the calling of monastic life, and who can serve as model for others. Through contact with him and by the effect of his personal influence, one will become a monk. Ascetic perfection does not suffice to create an *abba*; one must also be filled with the Spirit, endowed with discernment and the gift of speaking words which are adapted to the spiritual needs of each individual.[3] The number of spiritual men, of *abbates*, necessarily far surpasses that of spiritual fathers: it was only when disciples came to them that they became effective spiritual fathers.

The hierarchical and administrative connotation of the word *abba* comes only later. It is no doubt tied in with western ideas. In any case, it is linked with the organization of the monastic life.[4] There were no superiors in the anchoritic colonies of Lower Egypt and, in the first groupings, the superiors were not necessarily chosen from among the spiritual fathers. In other words, the superiors of the first monasteries were very often not abbots. According to the location, they were called overseer, father of the monastery, *senior qui praeest* and later on, in Greek, *archimandrite* and

2. Cf. I. Hausherr, *ib.*, p. 18–20.

3. Cf. J. Dupont, osb, "Le nom d'abbé chez les solitaires d'Egypte," *La Vie Spirituelle,* 77 (1947), 216.

4. Cf. L. Bouyer, *History of Christian Spirituality,* vol. 1: *The Spirituality of the New Testament,* New York, 1963, p. 515–516.

higoumene.[5] Nevertheless, there was no opposition between the spiritual father or *abba* and the holder of the governing power, simply because there never was any, in principle at least, between the spiritual men and the hierarchy. The governing officers themselves could also possess the Spirit. In fact, it did happen that an *abba* became superior when a group of disciples assembled around his cell; then he formed with them a *coenobium* and became their superior. It even came to pass that such an *abba* founded several *coenobia* and remained the sole superior;[6] but ordinarily, as a rule, the spiritual father and the *higoumene* were two distinct persons.

It is true that, later on, when monachism became organized, there tended to be an identification of the two functions, and there is no lack of examples of the *higoumene* being at the same time the spiritual father of his monks.[7] It is this latter function which seems the more stable. When an *higoumene* retires, he sometimes continues to direct his monks and remain their spiritual father.

Although the spiritual father was not a regular superior and did not have Holy Orders,[8] his sons regarded him with an absolute confidence and obedience. Once confidence had been placed in an *abba* or elder, it must not be withdrawn and given to another; otherwise there was the risk of falling into the danger of running from one director to another, thus tempting God and scandalizing men. Certain texts even go so far as to state that any doubt concerning the authority of the *abba* or the smallest criticism of his person or his actions constituted a grave sin. This fidelity in all trials was only possible through an unconditional obedience, a total submission: it is this which the ancient Fathers recommend

5. These two names will be synonymous until the sixth century; after this date, the latter will be reserved for the local superior of one single house.

6. Cf. J. M. Besse, *Les moines d'Orient antérieurs au concile de Chalcédoine* (451), Paris, 1900, p. 167–168.

7. Cf. I. Hausherr, "La direction spirituelle en Orient autrefois," *op. cit.*, p. 114–118.

8. The priesthood was by no means considered necessary for receiving a manifestation of conscience or for giving spiritual direction. In fact, spiritual fatherhood spread in the East chiefly in monastic settings which were purely lay so that it tended to become the heritage of the layman.

for our emulation.[9] Is this not the first hint of what will later be called the perpetuity of abbots? If the disciple must remain faithful to his master and the son to his spiritual father, and if he owes him, at the same time, an absolute submission, then at the moment when spiritual fatherhood and the charge of superior draw near to one another and, in fact, the two functions are united in the same person, it is logical and completely natural to consider that the superior, for his part, should be stable. The firmly imposed duty of obeying the elder whom one had previously chosen conferred on the latter a very real authority. Later on in organized communities, this authority could only belong fully to the *higoumene*. And finally, this authority, in order to be entirely and efficaciously exercised, should not be subject to change: it should always remain in the hands of the same superior as long as he lived.

The first monastic grouping under a cenobitical form of which history preserves some trace is that of Saint Pachomius. Formed in the anchoritic life, Pachomius, following a celestial intervention—as his biographer tells us—constructed a cell in Tabennesi about the year 315, where he received the recluses who wished to join him. This supernatural counsel could also have been accompanied by natural motives: the difficulties of the eremitical life and the advantages of the common life.[10] Pachomius accepted the recluses who desired to share his experience; he established a small *coenobium* and later founded a number of others. Because of this he had to draw up a constitution for the houses which were dependent on him; thus the problem of superior was posed. He himself, while remaining the "spiritual father" of his monks,[11] continued as head of the "congregation" all his life. Before he died he chose his successor, who in turn died three months later. Horsiesius, who succeeded him, established the one who should

---

9. Cf. I. Hausherr, "La direction spirituelle en Orient autrefois," *op. cit.,* p. 186–193.

10. Cf. P. Ladeuze, *Etude sur le cénobitisme pakomien pendant le IVe siècle et la première moitié du Ve,* Louvain, 1898, p. 165.

11. Cf. H. Bacht, "La loi du retour aux sources." "De quelques aspects de l'idéal monastique pachomien," *Revue Mabillon,* 51 (1961), 23.

preside over the group after him.[12] It should be mentioned, however, that Pachomius began by asking the brothers to designate the
one who should succeed him; but which was the deciding factor:
the choice of the brothers or that of the old abbot? In any case, the
authority of Pachomius was extensive. Theodore, before the
founder's death, had accepted the invitation of a group of elders to
assume the succession: Pachomius reproached him for this and
annulled the "election." Pachomius was also in conflict with the
bishop of the place who felt that he abused his authority by sending
away those monks whom he judged to be less worthy. It seems then
that the system which prevailed at Tabennesi was that of perpetuity for the superior of the congregation, with the appointment of successors.

It was otherwise for the overseers of the different houses. Named
by Pachomius and those who came after him, they remained
responsible to them and could be replaced, usually at the time of the
great assembly during the month of August or on the occasion of
the superior general's visitation of the houses.[13]

In the East, as in Egypt, it seems that the superior himself appointed his successor before he died: he was thus understood as
remaining in office all his life.[14] If he retired before his death, he
could proceed in the same way to the appointment of the one who
should replace him. Saint Basil concedes a great authority to the
superior, but nowhere does he speak of the duration of his charge.
There is even less information concerning what was done in the
monasticism of Palestine, Syria, Mesopotamia, and Constantinople
during the same period. We can simply venture to say that, at the

12. Cf. *Les Vies coptes de saint Pachome et de ses premiers successeurs*, trans. by
L. Th. Lefort (Bibliotheque du Museon vol. 16), Louvain, 1943, p. 48 and 272.

13. According to the text of Saint Jerome, at the great assembly in August,
"*disponuntur monasteriorum capita, dispensatores, praepositi, ministri, prout
necessitas postulaverit.*" Those who were in office at that time had to render an
account of their administration. Cf. A. Boon, *Pachomiana latina*, p. 8 and 95.

14. Cf. M. Besse, *Les moines d'Orient, op. cit.,* p. 170; P. De Meester, OSB,
*De monachico statu iuxta disciplinam byzantinam, Statuta selectis fontibus et com-
mentariis instructa* (S. Congregazione per la Chiesa Orientale. Codificazione
canonica orientale. Fonti, ser. II, fasc. X). Rome, 1942, p. 205–206.

outset of organized monasticism, the founder carried on a much
more extensive activity and enjoyed a very great degree of authority.
Besides this, even if he did not monopolize the spiritual direction
of his monks, he was usually their spiritual father and, under this
title, his prestige was vast and profound. As for the appointment of
superiors, there was as yet no precise juridical tradition to determine the conditions of the choice. Oftentimes it was the personality
of the candidate which asserted itself: by reason of his talents and
his virtue, the monks were in agreement about him. All of these
factors contributed to the establishment of perpetuity.

The excesses committed by the eastern monks of the fifth century
provoked a reaction on the part of the bishops. The Council of
Chalcedon in 451 places the monks under the jurisdiction and
surveillance of the diocesan bishop.[15] At the same time, it seeks to
limit the role and the activity of the monks. We will see the re-
percussions that this text had on the life of monasteries and the
regime of their superiors during the Middle Ages, even in the West.

The first formal text in the East concerning the election of abbots
for life by their community is an imperial constitution of 530 contained in the Justinian Code:

A Juliano pp sacris legibus nostris et hanc addendam esse nobis

15. Canon 4: "Those who lead a truly monachal life should be esteemed
as is fitting. But since certain ones, for whom the monastic life is merely a
pretext, stir up trouble in the affairs of Church and State, and travel from one
city to another without distinction, and even wish to build monasteries for
themselves alone, the Council has decided that no one will be able to build or
establish a monastery or church, in whatever location it might be, without the
consent of the bishop of the city; besides the fact that the monks of the country
and of the city are subject to the bishop, they should love peace, apply themselves only to fasting and prayer, and settle in the localities which are assigned
to them; they should not burden themselves with the affairs of the Church
or with temporal affairs, they should not take an interest in these and should
not leave their monastery except when the bishop of the city requests it in
case of necessity. . . . The bishop of the city should watch over the monasteries
in a very exacting manner." Hefele-Leclercq, *Histoires des Conciles,* II, 779.
On the trouble instigated by the monks in the East, cf. H. Bacht, "Die Rolle
des orientalischen Monchtums in der kirchenpolitischen Auseinandersett-
zungen um Chalkedon (451–519)," in A. Grillmeier-H. Bacht, *Das Konzil von
Chalkedon II,* Wurtzburg, 1953, p. 193–314.

visum est, quae ex virtute non ex temporis ordine pias prae-
fecturas concedit, ut in venerabilibus monasteriis vel asceteriis
nequaquam defuncto abbate vel abbatissa sequens vel secunda
succedant . . . sed quem et vita integra et honesti mores et
adsidua devotio (commendent) et totum reliquorum monachorum corpus vel maior eorum pars ad hoc idoneum putaverit et
propositis sanctis evangeliis elegerit, eum ad praefecturam
vocari. Si ergo proximus a defuncto idoneus et dignus est . . .
ille reliquis praeferatur. . . .[16]

Therefore, it is only on the death of the abbot that there is question
of appointing a successor, and this is incumbent on the community.
Whatever may be the authority of the bishop over the monks in
his diocese, he only has the right to confirm the newly elected
member. This is precisely stated in a *novella* from Justinian in 546:

Jubemus igitur abbatem aut archimandritam in unoquoque
monasterio ordinari non omnino secundum gradum monachorum, sed omnes monachi melioris opinionis existentes
eligant. . . . Sanctissimum autem episcopum, sub quo monasterium constitutum est, eum qui ita electus est omnibus modis
abbatem ordinare.[17]

Justinian thus defends the freedom and rights of the monasteries,
while he is the first to provide, for the East, an explicit juridical
text concerning the perpetuity of abbots. The Justinian Code had
the weight of law for the whole empire, including the West. It
is difficult to know to what extent it was applied. Nevertheless,
it perhaps explains the extension of the principle of the independence
of monasteries.

It seems that, in the West, monachism developed chiefly under
the cenobitical form, and it spread rapidly. Its existence is verified
in Italy, Gaul, Spain, and Africa from the middle of the fourth
century. As in the East, it consists essentially of laymen and,
although drawing inspiration from the ideals of the various institutions of Egypt and Asia, it does not confine itself to following any

16. 1, 3, *De episcopis et clericis,* n. 46; ed. Krueger, II, p. 33.
17. *Novella* 123, 34; ed. Shoell-Kroll, Berlin 1912, p. 618.

one of them. It very quickly occupies an important place and plays a conspicuous role in the Church. To get a clear idea of this, it is sufficient to observe the number of monks promoted to the epis-copate from the end of the fourth century and well into the fifth.[18] But this expansion of monachism and the fact that it gained a foot-hold in the Churches had its darker side. There soon was a definite rivalry between the clergy and the monks.[19]

As early as 401, an African Council assumes the defense of monasteries by forbidding the bishop to place at the head of a monastery in his diocese a monk who has come from another diocese.[20] This leaves us to suppose that the bishop at that time had certain rights with regard to the appointment or confirmation of the abbot, on condition that he did not choose from among the faithful who were under the jurisdiction of another diocese. A century later, however, the relations between bishops and monks were still not determined with any degree of precision, and they were far from being always peaceful. Although the Council of Carthage in 525 had declared itself in favor of the monks' in-dependence,[21] the question was raised again at Carthage in 536.

18. The texts which speak of these promotions only aim to assure the regularity of the procedure, especially that of election. Pope Siricius (384–399) considers this practice desirable. The Decree of Zosimus (ca. 420) requires a greater respect for the canonical resolutions relating to ordinations in general, but nowhere forbids monks access to the episcopacy. Only the Decree of Celestine I (ca. 432) to the bishops of southern Gaul is unfavorable to the preponderance of the monastic element in these provinces. It thus aims to curtail the tendency which Lerins had to assume a kind of monopoly in the recruiting of the Gallic episcopacy. "It is the condition of being an outside cleric, and in no way the monastic profession which constitutes for the monk an obstacle to his promotion to Orders and to the episcopacy." R. Oliger, *Les évêques réguliers,* p. 34–36 and 53. Due to the dearth of clerics and without prejudice to the established rules, Gelasius I (492–496) encourages the pro-motion of monks. However, this remains subordinate to the condition fixed by Celestine I, namely that there are no qualified candidates among the local clergy.

19. Cf. *Saint Martin et son temps, Studia Anselmiana,* 46, Rome, 1962.

20. Cf. The Council of Carthage in September 401, can. 13; cf. Mansi III, 971, and Hefele-Leclercq, II, 126.

21. This refers to the conflict between an Abbot Peter, superior of a monastery in the diocese of Carthage, and the Primate of Byzantium. The

The bishops confirmed the decision of 525,[22] and they added that the other monasteries should likewise enjoy the greatest amount of freedom, as far as the councils allowed. If they wish to have clerics ordained or oratories consecrated, it is up to the bishop of the place to perform the functions. In other spheres, the monasteries are independent of their bishop and owe him no sort of tenure:

> Oportet enim in nullo monasterio quemlibet episcopum cathedram collocare ; aut qui forte habuerint, habere ; nec aliquam ordinationem, quamvis levissimam facere, nisi clericorum, si voluerint habere ; esse enim debent monachi in abbatum suorum potestate. Et quando ipsi abbates de corpore exierint, qui in loco eorum ordinandi sunt, iudicio congregationis eligantur ; nec officium sibi huius electionis vindicet, aut praesumat episcopus.[23]

If there happens to be some dispute among the monks on the subject of the election, the other abbots will decide; if the difficulty persists, the matter will be brought before the primate of the province. This important text specifies the relations between the monks and the bishops; it also establishes the principle of free election of the abbot by his monks and his lifetime regime. Knowing the position that the African Churches held in the West at that time, it is possible to calculate the influence of this decision on the formation of law in the Latin Church.

---

abbot, a former sub-deacon in the latter diocese, had had recourse to the Primate for the ordination of clerics during the long vacancy of the See of Carthage which lasted eighteen years. The Primate laid claim to the monastery as dependent on him. When the abbot and his monks refused to comply with his unreasonable demands, the bishop excommunicated them. In his own defense, the abbot cites precedents and a text from Saint Augustine (*De moribus clericorum*, 1, II) where it is said that the monasteries founded by his disciples belong neither to the founders nor to the Church of Hippo, but to the community of monks. The Council of Carthage in 525 speaks out in favor of the abbot and affirms that the monks should be free from the jurisdiction of clerics. Hefele-Leclercq, II, 1072–1074.

22. Cf. Hefele-Leclercq, II, 1136.

23. Hardouin, II, 1178; Mansi, VIII, 841. Actually, we do not know whether this text was the subject of a synodal decision properly so called; it at least represents what Bishop Felician of Ruspe proposed to the assembly.

In Gaul, the conflict between monks and clergy seems to have been more animated and, naturally enough, the councils sided with the authority of the bishops. At Arles in 455, with regard to the rivalry between the monastery of Lerins and Theodore the diocesan bishop, the Fathers confirm the bishop's rights over ordinations, the confirmation of the newly baptized, and the admission to the monastery of clerics who are strangers to the diocese.[24] The Council of Agde in 506 prohibits the foundation or construction of a monastery without the permission of the bishop.[25] The First Council of Orleans in 511 decrees (can. 7) that abbots, priests, clerics and monks cannot solicit ecclesiastical goods from the princes without having been examined and approved by the bishop, and that the abbots are subject to the bishop who can correct them if they commit some fault against the rule.[26] The Council of Epaone in 517 goes even further than this: when an abbot has committed some misdeed, if he does not want to accept the successor whom the bishop appoints, the matter should be brought before the metropolitan.[27] This is equivalent to acknowledging the bishop's right to depose the abbot. Canon Two of the Fifth Council of Arles in 554 declares that the monasteries and the government of the monks fall under the jurisdiction of the diocesan bishop; it adds that he will also watch over prolonged absences of

24. "Hoc enim et rationis et religionis plenum est, ut clerici ad ordinationem episcopi debita subjectione respiciant; laica vero omnis monasterii congregatio ad solam ac liberam abbatis proprii, quem sibi ipsa elegerit ordinationem, dispositionemque pertineat; regula quae a fondatore ipsius monasterii dudum constituta est, in omnibus custodita." Hardouin, II, 781; Hefele-Leclercq, II, 886. The freedom of the election of abbots by the community is thus ack-- nowledged.

25. Canon 27; Hefele-Leclercq, II, 991.

26. Canon 19: "abbates pro humilitate religionis, in episcoporum potestate consistant et, si quid extra regolam faciunt, ab episcopo conrigantur." Maassen, *Concilia aevi merovingici,* Monumenta Germaniae Historica, 40, Scrip. rer. meroving. Concilia I, 1893, p. 7. Hefele-Leclercq, II, 1011–1013.

27. Canon 19: "Abbas si in culpa repperiatur aut fraude et innocentem se adserens ab episcopo suo accepere noluerit successorum, ad metropolitani iudicium deducatur." Massen, p. 24; Hefele-Leclercq, II, 1039.

the abbot.[28] Several councils anticipate the abbot's excommunication by the bishop in a certain number of cases.[29] The bishops were not sparing in their use of the extended authority that was thus conceded to them; some even overstepped the mark by excommunicating and deposing abbots as it suited them. The reaction did not delay in making itself felt, and it will be encouraged by Saint Gregory the Great.

Contemporary texts on monasticism are rather scarce, and often they do not speak of the abbot. The *Statuta sanctarum virginum* of Saint Cesarius of Arles foresee the free election of the abbess by the community, as well as the perpetuity of the charge:

> Quotiens sancta abatissa, ad Deum migraverit nulla ex vobis carnali affectu, aut pro natalibus aut pro facultatibus, aut pro parentela aliquam minus efficacem fieri velit ; sed omnes Christo inspirante unanimiter sanctam ac spiritalem eligite, quae ad regulam monasterii possit efficaciter custodire, et supervenientibus responsum cum aedificatione et compunctione et cum sancto affectu sapienter valeat reddere.[30]

There is no question of the bishop's intervention. The *Tertia Patrum Regula ad monachos,* on the contrary, insists on his authority and even foresees his intervention in certain instances. This Rule, written in Gaul at the beginning of the sixth century, follows very closely the Council of Agde conducted by Saint Cesarius in 506.[31] A curious document is the *Regula cuiusdam Patris ad monachos,*

---

28. Hefele-Leclercq, III, 170.

29. Cf. The Council of Orleans in 511, can. 7, Maassen, p. 4; the Council of Orleans in 533, can. 21, Maassen, p. 64; the Council of Orleans in 538, can. 26, Maassen, p. 81; the Council of Auxerre in 573–603, can. 26, Maassen, p. 182.

30. G. Morin, *S. Cesarii ep. Arelatensis Opera Omnia,* II. *Opera varia,* p. 117, 22.

31. "Si in vitio perstiterit (abbas), in notitiam episcopi deferatur; qui si ab episcopo correptus nec sic emendaverit, deponatur." Holstein, *Codex Regularum,* I, 22. It is the first case of a formal deposition by the bishop; however, it will only be pronounced in the second instance and if the abbot is incorrigible.

written in Gaul or in Italy in the fifth or sixth century and based
on Cassian and the Latin Basil.[32] It foresees the deposition of the
abbot who is incontinent, a drunkard, a "gyrovague," or possessed
of worldly morals, without any mention of the bishop's intervention. If the guilty one does not wish to submit his resignation it
is the monks who are authorized to leave the monastery, after
which the abbot will be excommunicated—presumably by the
bishop. Does not such a procedure imply that the abbot is by
right permanent and appointed for life and, on the other hand,
that no one has sufficient authority over him to oblige him to
leave? If the guilty one eventually repents, he must submit himself
to the elder who will have presided during the vacancy of the
office.

Furthermore, while reading these texts, especially those of the
Frankish councils, it must not be forgotten that the words "monastery," "monk," and "abbot" did not yet have the meaning which
they will later assume. It was still mainly a period of formation and
organization of the monastic life. In the sixth century in Gaul, the
abbot was usually the superior of a basilica, around which gravi-
tated a whole staff of persons resembling the population of a monastery properly so called.[33] This staff was often partly clerical for
the administration of the sacraments, and partly lay for the service
of prayer as well as the care of the sanctuary; it bore different names
which recall the many varied occupations. Accordingly, to the
extent that the abbot was in charge of a church, and that the community over which he presided was composed of clerics, he con-

32. "Si quis ex senioribus, sive is qui abbas nuncupatur, voluptuosus
existat, et ebriosus, et dives; et qui huic saeculo conformatur; id est, in curribus
et in equis de loco ad locum discurrat, hic non solum principatu fratrum
indignus est, verum etiam homicida animarum iudicandus est: et alius monasterio eius praeesse constituatur. Sin vero non poterint, monachi ab illo exeant,
et ille excommunicatur. Si vero poeniteat, subdat se sub manibus senioris, et
servituti se subjiciat, donec probaverit is qui praeest." Holstein, *Codex
Regularum,* Paris, 1663, II, 170.

33. Cf. Levillain, *Etudes sur l'abbaye de Saint-Denis à l'époque mérovingienne.*
II. *Les origines de Saint-Denis,* Library of the School of Paleography, 86 (1925),
52–62.

formed to the law that made him subject to the authority of the bishop. It was all the more necessary that these groups have no bond between them, not even that of a rule. Each followed the one of its choosing, or rather the one which had been laid down by the founder, whether it was a matter of an already existing rule or a new text. These rules, judging from the ones which have been preserved, were still primitive and not very detailed.

CHAPTER TWO

THE AGE OF THE BARBARIAN KINGDOMS

Sixth to Eighth Centuries

MONASTIC RULES

T HE FIRST MONKS in the West were often content to adopt one of the known eastern rules. Some monasteries did not even have a written rule: they followed the usages of another house that had a reputation for good observance. It is only in the sixth century that a legislative movement begins to take shape; yet in each country, and even in each district, monachism assumes a distinctive physiognomy. In the sixth century in southern and central Gaul, the Arlesian Rules predominate; the seventh century, on the contrary, is marked by the propagation of the Rule of Saint Columban. The Rule of Saint Benedict spread at a slower pace, especially outside of Italy, and for a time it was mixed with others, notably that of Saint Columban. It is not until the year 742 and the first Germanic council[1] that the Benedictine Rule is imposed on all the monks in Germany, when the Carolingian reform assured it a more extensive propagation.

The appointment of the abbot by his predecessor seems to have been a very widespread system in early times. It was the Pachomian custom and also that of the Egyptian monks.[2] Cassian reports that an anonymous abbot named as his successor a certain Patermutius;[3]

1. "Decrivimus . . . et ut monachi et ancille Dei monasteriales iuxta regulam sancti Benedicti ordinare et vivere, vitam propriam, gubernare studeant." Werminghoff, *Concilia aevi karolini, Monumenta Germaniae Historica*, Legum sectio V., 1886, I–I, p. 4, can. VII.

2. Cf. P. Ladeuze, *Etude sur le cénobitisme pakomien, op. cit.*, p. 286; and P. De Meester, *De monachico statu, op. cit.*, p. 216–218.

3. Cf. *Institutiones monachorum*, 4, 28.

and that the abbot Paphnucius provided for his succession.[4] If Faustus of Riez is to be believed, Honoratus did the same when he left Lerins for Arles.[5] In the second half of the fifth century, Lupician, before his death, names the abbots of his two monasteries in Jura.[6] In the sixth century, John of Réomé, and in the seventh century, Saint Columban and Landelin likewise regulate their succession.[7] Usually it is at the approach of death that the abbot appoints his successor; occasionally it is with a view toward retirement. The texts from Justinian cited above, prescribing an election and not the automatic accession of the "prior," are these not a reaction against the system of appointment by the predecessor? The legislative texts which support this latter system are rare in the West: the first appears to be that of the Council of Chalon held between 639 and 654.[8] Saint Benedict and Saint Gregory the Great, like Justinian and the Council of Carthage, are clearly not in favor of it; nevertheless, it will subsist up until the Carolingian Period and the beginnings of Cluny.[9] Besides, it was most coherent with a monarchical concept of government where the authority of the "most worthy," the founder or a man of exceptional character, asserted itself in a stable fashion by way of inheritance.

The appointment of a successor by the abbot in charge witnesses

---

4. Cf. *Collationes*, 4, 1.

5. Cf. Tillemont, *Mémoires pour servir à l'histoire ecclésiastique des six premiers siècles*, XV, p. 344, citing Eusebius, Homily 34.

6. *Vita Lupicini*, 12; AA. SS. March 21, p. 266.

7. Cf. *Dictionnaire d'Archéologie chrétienne et de Liturgie*, art. "Election abbatiale, 2616; and Mabillon, AA. SS. O.S.B., Paris 1668–1702, II, 875. This list can be completed by the examples given by T. P. McLaughlin, "Le très ancien droit monastique de l'Occident," *Archives de la France monastique*, XXXVIII, Ligugé, 1935, p. 91.

8. Canon 12: "Ut duo abbates in uno monasterio esse non debeant, ne sub obtentu potestatis semultas inter monachus et scandulum non generetur; verum tamen si quislibet abba sibi elegerit successore, ipsi qui eligitur, de facultatis ipsius monasterii ad regendum nullam habeat potestatem." Maassen, p. 210, can. 12.

9. Cf. T. P. McLaughlin, "Le très ancien droit monastique de l'Occident," *op. cit.*, p. 99 and n. 1. At Cluny, Berno and Aymard appoint their successors, cf. AA. SS. O.S.B. (Paris), V, 86 and 322.

C

in favor of the lifetime regime. In fact, it is at the approach of death that this appointment was normally made, as is explicitly stated in certain texts. Moreover, if the old abbot survived, he kept his complete authority, both spiritual and temporal, until he did finally die; it is only then that the successor came into office.

The Rule of the Master adopted this system: it is even the only one which legislates on the question in a precise manner. In chapter ninety-two, the Master states that the abbot should not set up a *secundarius*, that is a prior; he explains that this is in order to maintain the competition among the brothers and permit the abbot to see who will prove himself to be the best. When the abbot feels that his end is drawing near, he appoints the one who should succeed him[10] and he orders that the bishop be advised so that he may come and give his blessing; in the presence of the pontiff, he hands over to the chosen one the book of the Rule, the keys to the storehouses and treasury, the inventory of tools, pharmacopoeia and furniture, and he entrusts the community to his care.[11] The candidate thus appointed takes the place of the abbot, receives the bishop's blessing, deposits the book of the Rule on the altar, commends himself to the prayers of the pontiff, then gives the kiss of peace to all and entrusts the keys of the monastery to the cellarer. Finally, he goes to sit on the abbatial throne, *in cathedra sedeat predecessoris*, and all come to render their obedience, *deinde omnes eius genua osculentur*. He himself goes to give the kiss of peace to the old dying abbot who commends himself to the prayers of the new abbot. However, the Master foresees the case where the old abbot recuperates: at such a

10. "Et iam tempore mortis suae, vocatis omnibus ante se fratribus, dicat eis: Bene vos quidem omnes in observatione sancta egistis, bene acta vestra Dei semper praebuistis aspectibus; et vocato subito nomine illius, vel apprehensa manu eius, quem meliorem in omni perfectione semper absconse coeteris cavit, iudidicat omni congregationi: Audite me, filii, Trinitas sancta novit, cuius indicio hic eligitur, quia vobis omnibus in omni observatione mandatorum Dei . . . semper melior extiterit iste." Chapter 94 continues the discourse.

11. "De hoc breve gregis istius in iudicio Domini post me tu fracturus es rationem. Memento, frater, memento, quia plus cui creditur, plus ab eo exigitur . . . Abbas, ingredere oratorium Domini, et sta in loco meo cum congregatione iam tua."

time, he resumes all his rights and all his authority, with all the honors that are attached to it. The new abbot can do nothing more than await his death. The most astonishing fact is that the author of this Rule still allows the old abbot the possibility of changing his mind and appointing another successor. After such a solemn nomination, after the bishop's blessing and the installation, if he decides that the appointed candidate is not the best, he can choose another.[12] Chapter ninety-four is devoted to the case where the abbot dies suddenly without having time to choose a successor. The selection will then be made by a *sanctissimus* abbot designated by the bishop of the place and his clergy. What should be remembered in this extraordinary procedure is that, for the Master, the abbatial functions truly cease only with death since, even after having chosen his successor and having had him blessed and installed, the abbot can change all this before he dies.

If Saint Benedict was familiar with this text, he has retained none of it. Not only does he avoid endorsing the appointment of a successor by the abbot in charge, but he formally declares himself in favor of election by the community. As has been seen, this system existed before his time: he has only made it more precise. Other than this, from the three cases considered in his Rule, as well as from the whole of chapters two and sixty-four, nothing can be concluded about the duration of the abbatial charge. The bishop of the place, the neighboring abbots and the faithful of the area can intervene to depose an unworthy abbot either at the time of his election or after he will have proven himself unqualified for the task. But that is perfectly compatible with the principle of a lifetime abbatial charge. In order to complete the given facts of the Rule with the information offered by Saint Gregory the Great in his Life of Saint Benedict, it should be noted that the holy Patriarch

12. "Et mox sciat pro certo, quia cum abbas frequenter in aliquas culpass quem elegerat, non in maius proficientem, sed per negligentiam magis deterioratum eum aspexerit, et monitus ab abbate non emendaverit se: et nomen eius deleat . . . de diptico . . .; a latere iam deiungatur abbatis; et ex illa iam die ab abbate alius frater . . . quaeratur . . . qui et ispe electus absconse, quotidie tempore mortis suae manu sua abbas eum apertius iudicet. . . ."

twice renounced the government of his community. He first left a monastery where the monks had wanted to poison him; then he withdrew from Subiaco to go and found Monte Cassino.[13] But these resignations do not encroach on the principle of perpetuity; they are merely the testimony of an age when the juridical bond uniting the abbot with his monastery was not yet clearly defined, and when spiritual freedom, by means of such relinquishments, sought to flee from a definite evil or to realize what appeared, in these exceptional circumstances, to be a greater good.

THE TESTIMONY OF HAGIOGRAPHY

From the most ancient times, as seen in the case of Saint Benedict, some abbots voluntarily relinquished their functions. A certain number left the government of their community in order to live a more retired existence in a greater and more austere solitude, others in order to be free to realize the projects that were dear to them, and still others for reasons of health or old age.

The *Vita Sancti Samsonis* (d. 565) relates that this holy personage, having been made abbot of his monastery, left it to follow certain Scots who were coming from Rome and re-entering their own country. Having returned to his monastery, he left it anew to retire into solitude. Appointed abbot of another monastery by a synod, he finally became bishop of Dole in Brittany.[14] Saint Columban (ca. 540–615) founded Annegray, Luxeuil, Fontaines-en-Vosgues, and Bobbio: he was abbot of these different monasteries and perhaps retained the title, but it is obvious that he could not govern them all together. Saint Benedict Biscop (628–689), already a monk, goes on pilgrimage to Rome and, on his way back, enters Lerins.[15] Having returned to his own country by order of the pope, he is made abbot of Saint Peter of Canterbury. He resigns and goes again to Rome. On his return, he founds the monastery of Wear-

13. Saint Gregory, second book of *Dialogues,* ch. 3 and 8.
14. Cf. Mabillon, AA. SS. O.S.B. (Solesmes), I, 174–176.
15. Cf. Mabillon, AA. SS. O.S.B. (Solesmes), II, 1003–1005.

mouth where he becomes the abbot. Saint Sigram (d. 650), abbot of Laurey in the country of Bourges, resigns, as his biographer tells us, in order to live in *peregrinus*, in voluntary exile and in a greater poverty, while carrying on a fisherman's trade.[16] Saint Germer (d. c. 658), having entered the monastery of Pentale in Normandy, becomes its abbot. According to his biographer,[17] after some violation he retires into solitude and lives in a cave; ordained priest, he founds a new monastery at Flay near Beauvais. Saint Filibert (d. 684), abbot of Rebais, leaves this monastery after a revolt of his monks—as the author of his life recounts[18]—and, after having visited various monasteries, founds the abbey of Jumièges and also Noirmoutier; he dies after having resigned from office. Saint Riquier, first abbot of Centule, goes to preach the faith to the Bretons beyond the seas, then re-enters his monastery and becomes a hermit, *"quatenus liberius soli Deo vacaret et contemplativos carperet fructus."*[19] The *Vita sancti Mederici* or Merry (d. c. 700), abbot of Autun, relates that this holy personage retired into solitude,[20] but that the bishop made him return in order to ordain him a priest; after which he again departed, went to Paris where he stayed at the monastery of Campelle, then at Melun, at Charenton, and lastly at La-Celle-saint-Pierre where he died. Saint Hermeland

16. Cf. Mabillon, AA. SS. O.S.B. (Solesmes), II, 414; complete text in *Analecta Bollandiana*, III, 379–406. The *Vita* is from the ninth century.

17. Cf. Mabillon, AA. SS. O.S.B. (Solesmes), II, 479.

18. "Quia perfecti viri semper perfectiora sectantur, coepit sacerdos Domini sanctorum coenobia circuire, ut aliquid emolumenti ex susceptione sanctitatis valeret accipere." AA. SS. O.S.B. (Solesmes), II, 822; M.G.H., Scr. Rer. Merov., *Vitae Sanctorum*, V, p. 587, 3. As can be seen, this author deems it more perfect to visit other monasteries than to remain in one's own, especially when one is abbot.

19. Mabillon, AA. SS. O.S.B. (Solesmes), II, 194. The author then recalls the example of Mary "sedente secus pedes eius et verbum vitae attentius audiente . . . monasticam vitam petiit, quo secretius sola caelestia mente rimaretur, Ecclesiae regimen alteri (abbati) tradens. . . ."

20. "Cum iam dictus b. confessor votis esset martyr, quia non constat martyrium in sola gladii peremptione, at vitiorum concupiscentiarumque crucifixione; non credens sibi integrum esse praemium, si inter tantam multitudinem vitam duxisset. . . ." Mabillon, AA. SS. O.S.B. (Solesmes), III–I, 12–13.

(d. 720), abbot of Aindre near Nantes, having reached an advanced age, retires to devote himself to a more solitary life.[21] Saint Herefrid, abbot of Lindisfarne, became a hermit before his death in 747.[22] Saint Austrulf's biographer tells us that this abbot of Fontenelle left his monastery after six years of governing to go on pilgrimage to Rome and, on his way back, he died at Agaune.[23] Saint Dado was already a hermit before he founded the monastery of Conques and became abbot in about 755; once the community was thriving sufficiently, he retired to live again as a hermit.[24]

According to our sources, the number of abbots who resign for reasons of health is less great. For the same period, there is mention of Saint Ursmer, abbot of Lobbes (d. 713), who retires with the consent of his monks because of sickness and old age.[25] Saint Wando, abbot of Fontenelle, overcome by gout and blindness, retires four years before his death.[26] Saint Wunebald, abbot of

21. "Cum ad senilem venisset aetatem," he builds for himself a small oratory where, with the king's permission, he retires with four brothers: "in quo relicto pastoralis curae regimine . . . ipse deinceps se retrusit, ut ab omni non solum superfluae, quin etiam justae curae inquietudine exutus, libere in theoricis Domini soli vacaret studiis." Mabillon. AA. SS. O.S.B. (Solesmes), III–I, 396, and M.G.H., *Script. rer. meroving.*, V, *Passiones Vitaeque SS.*, p. 70, I, I.

22. Cf. AA. SS. Boland., October XIII, 852.

23. "Accensus igne divini amoris, partibus Romuleae urbis ad limina beatorum Apostolorum Petri et Pauli iter disposuit: convocatisque fratribus, devotionem quam animo conceperat liquido promisit. Tunc omnes unius vocis clamore haec contradicunt, dicentes se nunquam eum desertures. E contra ille causa suae salutis et illorum, corpore humi prostratus, profecturum se velle proclamabat. Quid multa? Videns universa caterva fratrum flebilibus eius precibus se obviare non posse, conticuit, piique Patris petitionibus cessit. Demum benedictione percepta, omnibus fratribus pacis osculum dedit. . . ." Mabillon, AA. SS. O.S.B. (Paris), III–II, 135. What should be retained from this whole little scene is the fact that the bond which unites the abbot with his community is henceforth confirmed.

24. Cf. G. Desjardins, *Cartulaire de Conques*, Paris, 1879, p. 509–511.

25. Cf. Mabillon, AA. SS. O.S.B. (Solesmes), III–I, 242 and 566; M.G.H., *Scrip. rer. merov.*, VI (445), 464, 7; *ib.*, different text, 460, 15.

26. Cf. Mabillon, AA. SS. O.S.B. (Paris), III–2, 132, 4; M.G.H., *Scrip. rer. merov.*, II, 286. Before retiring, he appoints his prior to succeed him, with the consent of the community.

Heidenheim, retires from office because of infirmity three years before his death in 761.[27]

There are two instances of abbots having to leave their monastery for political reasons: Wala, abbot of Corbie, died in exile at Bobbio in 835, and Ambrose Autpertus, abbot of Saint Vincent at Volturno, left his charge only a year after his election.[28] Two others resign without any motive being given by their biographers: Saint Eleutherius of Spoleto[29] and Saint Bertin, abbot of Sithiu. Is it necessary to add that all of these testimonies are given as furnished by the sources, but a certain number of them are more recent than the heroes of the legends which recount their *mirabilia;* above and beyond the authenticity of all these events and all the given motivations, they vouch for the fact that abbatial resignation is not uncommon and that it poses no difficulty.

Until the ninth century, we are not aware of the conditions under which these resignations took place. Certain texts mention the approval of the community, others that of the king or the proprietor; the approval of the diocesan bishop should no doubt be added, as is explicitly foreseen in the Penitential attributed to Theodore for England of the seventh and eighth centuries.[30] Gradually, the bonds which unite the abbot and his community are reinforced and made more precise.

THE INFLUENCE OF THE POPES

Pelagius I (555–560) confirms the principle of election for abbots and brings to bear an important precision. The abbot should be

27. Cf. Mabillon, AA. SS. O.S.B. (Paris), III–2, 185.

28. Cf. J. Winandy, O.S.B., *Ambroise Autpert,* Paris 1953, p. 27.

29. Cf. Saint Gregory the Great, *Dialogues* III, 33 (PL 77:296); and Mabillon, AA. SS. O.S.B. (Solesmes), I, 289.

30. N. 64: "Abbati scilicet monasterium suum alii dare in potestate non est, nec post obitum eius, nec eo vivente sine voluntate monachorum, nec propinquo nec alieno, sed ipsi eligant sibi abbatem. Si Prior obierit, aut discesserit, simili modo. Abbas potest pro humilitate, cum permissione episcopi, locum suum derelinquere. Tamen fratres eligant sibi abbatem de ipsis, si habent; sin autem, de extraneis. Nec episcopus debet violenter in loco suo. Congregatio

chosen by the monks of the community which he is called upon to
govern, in agreement with the proprietor of the monastery, if
there is a proprietor outside of the community; then the proper
steps will be taken for his "ordination," that is, his installation and
benediction by the bishop of the place.[31] The Pope adds in another
letter:

> nullam potestatem de caetero, nullam licentiam monachis
> relinquentes pro arbitrio suo aut expellere abbates aut sibimet
> alios ordinare. . . .[32]

This is not a promulgation of the lifetime abbatial regime, but it is
the elimination of one of the causes which could be opposed to it.
If the monks elect their abbot, are they not also able to depose him?
That is the question to which the pontifical decision responds. In
setting aside this most dangerous cause of instability in the abbatial
office, the text of Pelagius I effectively contributes to assure the
perpetuity of abbots. The worth of these two texts was well perceived in former times: they have been inserted in the great collections of Canon Law and are found again in the Decree of Gratian.[33]

The legislation of Saint Gregory the Great completes that of
Pelagius I. If the canon of the Roman Synod of 595 is a forgery,[34]

---

debet sibi eligere abbatem post mortem eius, aut eo vivente, si discesserit, vel
peccaverit. . . ." P. W. Finsterwalder, *Die Canones Theodori Cantuariensis und
ihre Ueberlieferungsformen,* 1929, p. 319–320.

31. "Abbatem autem in eodem loco illum volumus ordinari, quem sibi de
sua congregatione et monachorum electio et possessionis dominus, et quod
magis observandum est, ordo vitae ac meritum poposcerit ordinari." Jaffe,
987. Critical text established by P. Gasso-C. Battle O.S.B., *Pelagii Papae I
epistulae quae supersunt* (556–561), (Scripta et documenta 8, Montserrat, 1956),
83. According to Gasso, this text would depend on the Rule of Saint Benedict.

32. Letter of Pelagius I, "*Opilioni defensori.*" P. Gasso-C. Battle, *ib.,* 116–118;
Jaffe, 1001.

33. *Decretum,* c. XVIII, qu. 2, c. 4 and 9.

34. "Defuncto . . . abbate, non extraneus eligatur, nisi de eadem congregatione, quem sibi propria voluntate concors fratrum . . ." Jaffe, 1366; cf.
McLaughlin, "Le très ancien droit monastique de l'Occident," *op. cit.,*
p. 177–186.

the letter to the Bishop of Rimini is authentic. The Pope establishes that the Ordinary of the place has only the right to ordain the one chosen by community vote on the death of the predecessor:

> Castorio fratri et coepiscopo nostro . . . illa videlicet ei iurisdictione relicta, ut in defuncti abbatis locum alium quem dignum communis consensus congregationis elegerit, debeat ordinare.[35]

In a letter to Marinianus, Bishop of Ravenna, Saint Gregory likewise writes:

> Defuncto vero abbate non extraneus nisi de eadem conversatione quem sibi propria voluntate congregatio elegerit, et qui electus fuerit sine dolo vel venalitate aliqua ordinetur.[36]

He expresses himself in the same vein in his missive to the monasteries of Autun.[37] Saint Gregory insists on election by the community, or at least on the necessity of their approval, to check against the unwarranted interference of outsiders in the life of the monastery, especially against the pretensions of the bishops;[38] but he never fails to indicate that this election should take place only on the death of the predecessor. The bishop certainly has the power to depose an abbot, but this is only when the latter is guilty of a grave fault, and he must act in conformity with the canons. With respect to this fact, the Pope uses a very strong expression in support of perpetuity:

> Neque viventi abbate quaecumque persona qualibet occasione in suo monasterio praeponatur, nisi forte exstantibus . . . criminibus, quae sacri canones puniri monstrantur.[39]

35. M.G.H., *Epistolae,* I, 346 (Epist. V, 47).

36. M.G.H., *Epistolae,* II, 19 (Epist. VIII, 17).

37. "Item constituimus, ut obeunte abbate atque presbytero suprascripti xenodochii atque monasterii, nisi quem rex eiusdem provinciae eum consensu monachorum secundum Dei timorem elegerit ac praeviderit ordinandum." M.G.H., *Epistolae,* II, 377 (Epist. XIII, 11).

38. Cf. The letter cited above to the Bishop of Rimini, and the one to the Bishop of Urbe Veteri (Orvieto), M.G.H., *Epistolae,* I, 13 (Epist. I, 12).

39. M.G.H., *Epistolae,* II, 19 (Epist. VIII, 17).

The Pope recognizes that the bishop holds jurisdiction over the monasteries of his diocese, and that he can punish an unworthy abbot or depose an incompetent one; but he has not the right to depose him without just cause.[40] It happens that Saint Gregory directly intervenes to depose some abbots and appoint their successors;[41] by this action, he affirms the supreme authority of the Roman Pontiff, but he does not intend to infringe on the principle of perpetuity.

With regard to culpable abbots, if the fault is anterior to the election, Saint Gregory pronounces the deposition and prescribes a new election.[42] But when a regularly ordained abbot is found to be at fault after his ordination, he hesitates to remove him from office. This is seen in the case of three abbots of whom there is question in the letters to Venantius, Bishop of Luni, and Constance, Bishop of Milan.[43] Two were priests, the third a deacon. The Pope is opposed to their reinstatement in Holy Orders but, after a time of penance, the first will be able to go to a monastery chosen by the bishop where he will occupy the first rank among the monks; the second will be able to re-enter his own monastery, always in the first rank of monks; the third will resume the government of his monasteries of Gorgonia and Capraria. The case of the abbot from the monastery of Saint Theodore in Palermo is similar:[44] after a long period of penance, the bishop will authorize him to resume the government of his monastery, but the Pope appoints a sort of coadjutor in the person of a *praepositus*. It seems that, for Saint Gregory, abbatial election and ordination were acts which could only be annulled with great difficulty. The lifetime dignity which

40. M.G.H., *Epistolae*, I, 284, 298, 299 (Epist. V, 4, 17, 18); and II, 424 (Epist. XIV, 6).

41. This is the case of the letter to Fortunatus, Bishop of Naples, where he asks him to ordain the candidate whom he has appointed to replace the overseer of a monastery, M.G.H., *Epistolae*, II, 49 (Epist. IX, 12) and the case of his intervention with regard to the abbot, Urbicus, in 598; M.G.H., *Epistolae*, II, 54 (Epist. IX, 20).

42. Cf. M.G.H., *Epistolae*, I, 181 (Epist. III, 23).

43. Cf. M.G.H., *Epistolae*, I, 298, 299 (Epist. V, 17, 18).

44. Cf. M.G.H., *Epistolae*, I, 284 (Epist. V, 4).

adorned the abbots made them difficult to replace. However, not
everyone shared these ideas with Gregory.[45]

The great Pope also intervenes in another very different manner.
He favored the interruption of the abbatial charge for promotion
to the episcopate. Saint Gregory was convinced of the incompati-
bility of the clerical way of life with the monastic way of life, but
the pressing needs of the Church often led him to entrust to monks
and abbots the government of dioceses. He chooses bishops without
discrimination from the ranks of the clergy and from the monasteries. Sometimes, to allow the candidate to better prepare himself,
he even orders him to enter a monastery; it might then be said that
he considers monastic life to be an excellent preparation for the
episcopate.[46] But to prevent the monasteries and monastic life from
suffering because of these promotions, the Pope sternly prohibits
the pluralism of combining the abbatial office with the episcopate,
and he charges that all monks and abbots elevated to ecclesiastical
dignity should absent themselves from their community. Every
election which has been accepted and ratified by the abbot entails,
for the chosen one, the loss of rights and powers which he had in
his monastery. For example, in two freedom charters concerning
the monasteries of Autun founded by Queen Brunhilda, Gregory
solemnly forbids the abbots to accept the episcopate if they have
not previously renounced their charge, *nisi deposita abbatia,* and
before they have been given a successor.[47] The custom of en-
trusting the government of churches to monks, so liberally en-

45. Witness to this fact is canon 17 of the Latunensian Council in 673–675:
"Episcopos vero seu abbates, qui propriis culpis notanter damnati sunt aut ab
ecclesiis eorum sponte remoti sunt, nullo modo ad proprias ecclesias vel
onores decrevimus revertendos." Maassen, p. 219.

46. Cf. Oliger, *Les évêques réguliers, op. cit.,* p. 42.

47. Jaffe, 1875; M.G.H., *Epistolae,* II, 376 (Epist. XIII, 11). Cf. Oliger, *Les
évêques réguliers,* p. 44, note. Completely different is the case of Ireland where
it is the abbots who represent the hierarchy, while the bishops are simple
monks destined to perform ordinations; and also the case of the claustral
bishops in Gaul and that of missionary bishops in the Frankish and Germanic
countries. All of these bishops could combine the episcopate with monastic
life and even with the abbatial charge; cf. Oliger, *ib.,* p. 18 and 21; L.
Gougaud, *Les chrétientés celtiques,* Paris, 1911, p. 219.

couraged by Saint Gregory, became generalized again in the course of the two centuries which followed his pontificate. In the ninth century, Pope Nicholas I will condemn the custom of electing to episcopal sees monks from another church; but he will in no way be opposed to the principle of promoting monks.[48]

It was seen earlier that the Merovingian Councils of the first half of the sixth century declared themselves in support of the bishops against the rights of the abbots, and that this resulted in the very frequent deposition of abbots by their bishop. The councils of the second half of the sixth century, shortly after the Justinian Code and the Council of Carthage in 536, and those of the seventh century, legislated against such an abuse which infringed on the autonomy of the monastic life as well as the perpetuity of abbots. The Council of Tours, held in 567, forbids the bishops to depose an abbot without having assembled a synod of abbots, from whom they should request counsel.[49] The Council of Paris in 614 (or 615) establishes that, if an abbot has been deposed in an unorthodox fashion, he has the right to appeal before the synod.[50] Another council held shortly after 614 comes back to the question and declares that abbots cannot be removed from office unless there is a grave fault on their part.[51]

THE ROLE OF FOUNDERS, PRINCES AND MAGNATES

In former times, monasteries were more often founded by lay-

48. Cf. Oliger, *Les évêques réguliers,* p. 46 and 62.

49. Canon 7: "Ut episcopus nec abbatem nec archipresbyterum sine omnium suorum cumpresbyterorum et abbatum concilio de loco suo praesumat eiecere neque per premium alium ordinare nisi facto concilio tam abbatum quam presbyterorum suorum. . . ." Maassen, p. 124.

50. Canon 4: "Salubriter consilio unianimi instituemus observandum, ut, si episcopus, quod non credimus esse venturum, aut per iracundia, quod esse non debet, aut per pecunia abbatem, quia fratres nostri sunt, de loco suo eiecerit non canonice, ille abbas recurrat ad synodum. Et quia fragilis esse nostra natura videtur, si episcopus, qui eum eiecit, ab hac luce migraverit, successor eius abiectum fratrem revocet ad sedem." Maassen, p. 187.

51. Canon 11: "Ut abbatis, archipresbyteri absque culpas de ecclesiastico ministerio removeri non debeant. . . ." Maassen, p. 195.

men, princes and noblemen, or by bishops, than by monks; such persons had an abundance of material resources. These founders established the monastery on grounds which belonged to them and, as the canons required, endowed it with lands and houses. But by virtue of a kind of natural or common right, perhaps influenced in certain areas by the Germanic custom, they continued to have, with regard to their foundation, an attitude which could veer from simple protection to intervention in the temporal administration or the abbatial appointment. They even went so far as to entirely dispose of the property, which they would present as a gift to another religious institution or to another individual. The founders often thought of their foundation as still belonging to them in a certain way. The monastery is then appropriated and the proprietor sees it as part of his patrimony. However, the monastery is itself a moral person, able to acquire and possess; it is a juridical person. The exercise of the right of property on this estate is thus limited and it cannot be considered as a *dominium* in the strict sense of the word. A monastery which has been appropriated can enjoy electoral freedom if the privilege is expressly accorded to it.[52]

The Church has acknowledged this situation. In Spain the Council of Lerida, held in 524 or 546, recognizes the rights of the founder. When he has a church built, he is the one who has it consecrated, and if he destines it for a monastery, it is exempt from the bishop; the text of the canon adds that this will be so even if there are as yet no monks and no rule has been set up for them by the bishop—which clearly shows that the rights over this church could only belong to the proprietor.[53] The Ninth Council of Toledo held in 655 is more explicit and more attentive to detail. It foresees the founder's right to present the abbot to the bishop who should ordain him, without reference to any intervention on the part of

52. Cf. McLaughlin, "Le très ancien droit monastique," *op. cit.,* p. 238–245; Levy-Bruhl, *Les élections abbatiales,* p. 185–186; and U. Berlière, *Les élections abbatiales au moyen âge,* Bruxelles, 1927, p. 13–15.

53. Canon 3: ". . . ubi congregatio non colligitur vel regula ab episcopos constituitur." Hefele-Leclercq, II, 1064, This text will appear in the *Corpus Juris Canonici,* C. XVI, q. I, c. 34 and c. X, q. I, c. I.

the community. However, it is not certain that this right was also recognized in the case of proprietors.[54] In Gaul, the councils in many places assume the rights of the founder and the proprietor over abbatial elections.[55] In Italy, Pope Pelagius I, writing in 559 to the sub-deacon, Melleus, in Lucania, prescribes that "he will be empowered to act as abbot whom the monks and the proprietor will have chosen from among the former."[56] During the Lombard period, the rights of the proprietor are generally recognized.[57] On the other hand, Saint Gregory does not speak of it, and he does not conceal his preference for election by the community alone, in conformity with the Rule of Saint Benedict. He upholds monastic immunities. And he had to struggle to assure the freedom of the abbatial election, in Italy at least. In Gaul he does not intervene in these matters. In the East, Byzantine monachism has also recognized the rights of the founder, even understood in a broader sense, over the designation of the *higoumene;* and these rights were transmissible by inheritance, by contract or even by prescription.[58]

In the West the usurpation of abbeys by the laity does not happen in one stroke. It even seems that, during the Merovingian period, the rights of the founder and those of the proprietor have not yet led to a vast appropriation of monasteries by secular hands; that will result from the combination of factors which is called feudalism. It is rare enough at that time for a monastery to be owned by a layman. It seems that each time a layman gives away a monastery as his own property, it is in the role of founder, and he disposes

---

54. Canon 2: ". . . fundatores ecclesiarum atque rectores idoneos in eisdem basilicis iidem ipsi offerant episcopis ordinandos." Bruns, *Canones Apostolorum et conciliorum saec. IV, V, VI, VII,* Berlin 1839, I, 292; Hefele-Leclercq, III, 292. The context indicates that here it is a question of monasteries as well as secular churches.

55. Cf. McLaughlin, "Le très ancien droit monastique," *op. cit.,* p. 245.

56. Cf. P. Gasso–C.M. Battle, *Pelagii I Papae epistulae quae supersunt* (556–561), (Scripta et documenta 8, Montserrat, 1956), p. 83.

57. Cf. Grasshoff, *Langobardisch-frankisches Klosterwesen in Italien,* p. 57; and Voigt, *Koningliche Eigenkloster in Langobardinreich,* Gotha, 1909, p. 111.

58. Cf. P. De Meester, *De monachico statu, op. cit.,* p. 139, 218–219.

of it in favor of another abbey of the house which he has created.[59]

The king in the Merovingian period does not intervene in the nominations made by the proprietors. He appoints the abbots of his own abbeys and leaves the other proprietors to make use of their rights. The king's action only makes itself felt indirectly with regard to the other abbeys, and rather in support of monastic immunities.[60]

As for the diocesan bishop, he originally held no rights over the monastic society as society because of the fact that it was composed solely of laymen. It was only from the moment when it was considered to be a "religious" society that he had some right of control over it. The Church's legislation, in fact, considers the obligations of the monk as ecclesiastical obligations, and on certain points likens him to the cleric.[61] From the sixth century, the bishops took on the practice of giving a special blessing to abbots, chiefly in Great Britain and in Gaul; at about the same period, this custom, joined to the promotion of abbots to the priesthood, contributed toward giving the bishops a great influence over abbatial elections.[62] Later on, the accession of monks to the body of clergy only served to extend the rights of the diocesan heads over the monasteries. But it was chiefly the appropriation of abbeys by the bishops which laid the foundation of their right to intervene in the election of abbots; often they proceeded to the appointment of the latter. Again it must be noted that the vocabulary and the institution itself were not very precise. Even in what was called "election" by the community, the role of the latter could be sufficiently diminished and consist mainly in passive acceptance of the presentation or appointment made by the bishop or the proprietor. In any case, it was the bishop's duty to install or ordain the abbot, that is, to

59. Cf. E. Lesne, *Histoire de la propriete ecclesiastique,* Paris, 1910–1943, I, p. 136.

60. Cf. H. Levy-Bruhl, *Les élections abbatiales, op. cit.,* p. 187.

61. Cf. McLaughlin, "Le très ancien droit monastique," *op. cit.,* p. 112–114.

62. Cf. Levy-Bruhl, *Les élections abbatiales, op. cit.,* p. 62 and 66; McLaughlin, "Le très ancien droit monastique," *ib.,* p. 137.

confirm him and put him in charge, which is what he did by conferring a liturgical blessing.[63] It is probably in this sense that we
should understand canon 51 of the Fourth Council of Toledo (633)
which will be recalled by Gratian in this Decree:[64]

> Hoc tantum sibi in monasteriis vindicent sacerdotes, quod
> praecipiant canones, id est monachos ad conversationem sanctam
> praemonere, abbates aliaque officia instituere atque extra
> regulam acta corrigere.[65]

It remains that the bishop had the right to punish culpable abbots,
have them confined to another monastery, and even depose them,
as has been seen above.[66] He had another right which was gradually
confirmed and made more precise: that of authorizing the abbot
to resign in order to retire to another monastery, to accept the
charge of another house, or to become a hermit. The bishop then
had numerous motives for intervening in the life of the abbeys
and the regime of their superiors. Founder's rights, protection,
proprietor's rights, ecclesiastical jurisdiction: he could invoke all of
these titles.[67] In fact, the interference of the bishops was extensive.
Beyond the causes enumerated above, it was justified by the fact
that, at this time, the abbeys were populated by communities which

63. McLaughlin, *ib.*, p. 88, 92, 97.

64. Caus. XVIII, q. II, c. I.

65. Cf. Hardouin, III, 575. The *sacerdotes* referred to here are the bishops.
Levy-Bruhl, *Les élections abbatiales, op. cit.*, p. 29 and Perez de Urbel, *Les
monjes espanoles*, Madrid, II, p. 49, think that the Spanish bishops at that time
had the right to name all the abbots of their diocese. This is true in the numerous episcopal monasteries and in the strictly monastic houses where they
were the founders or the proprietors; in the others, the bishop designated
the abbot, but the community could elect him, in the old sense, by ratifying
the presentation. If the Spanish councils insist on the rights of the bishop, it is
not in opposition to those of the community, but against the pretensions of
secular lords.

66. See pp. 10-11. The Pact of Saint Fructuosus of Braga foresees, at the
request of the monks, an intervention of the bishop, of neighboring abbots,
and of the Count, in case of shortcomings on the part of the abbot; but the
text does not mention deposition. Cf. PL 87:1128.

67. Cf. E. Lesne, *Histoire de la propriété ecclésiastique, op. cit.*, I, p. 137.

were more or less regular and were centered around basilicas which depended on the local churches. It is only from the moment when the regular character of these establishments is confirmed, that is from approximately the eighth century, that the abbeys, unless they were owned by the bishops, had nothing more to fear from the latter's control, especially where electoral freedom and abbatial perpetuity were concerned.[68]

If it has thus been established that during the whole of the High Middle Ages numerous abbots did abandon their charge and their monasteries it is merely a statement of fact, because certain circumstances motivated these infractions contrary to the principle of the lifetime regime.

68. Cf. Levy-Bruhl, *Les élections abbatiales, op. cit.,* p. 83.

D

CHAPTER THREE

THE CAROLINGIAN PERIOD AND ITS
CONSEQUENCES

Ninth and Tenth Centuries

DURING THE COURSE OF THE EIGHTH century, while the abbey is still seen as an establishment set apart for religious purposes, it will be considered more and more as a piece of real estate producing revenues. Monasteries at that time were composed of huge estates which were constantly being augmented; it was inevitable that they should stimulate covetousness. Charles Martel's struggle against the Mohammedans obliged him to recruit fighters whom he had to pay. In order to do this, he distributed among them Church lands and monasteries. These new proprietors considered their monasteries as a legacy from which profit was to be derived. At times of abbatial nominations, they were inspired more by their own self-interests than by the interests of the community. In this way, the abbatial office tended to assume political worth; abbeys were entrusted to persons who had no other claims than those of services rendered to royalty. It was at this time that royal power imposed the obligation of fidelity on the abbots; later on, they will become genuine officials, residing at the court and charged with duties and missions. As the prince's "faithful," they are required to serve by their person, by their influence, and by their material goods. Under these conditions, the royal power does not hesitate to depose them when they no longer correspond to what is expected of them.[1] At the same time the king more and more becomes the proprietor of the

---

1. Cf. H. Levy-Bruhl, *Les élections abbatiales, op. cit.,* p. 91.

monasteries, and not only those which have surrendered themselves, by way of *tuitio,* to be protected by him. He can certainly concede to the monks the right to elect their abbot; but in fact, at the end of the eighth century and into the ninth, it is rare that the monks enjoy electoral freedom in royal abbeys—and there is hardly any other kind. One may catch a glimpse of the consequences: henceforth the king regularly intervenes to elect or to depose the abbots. And he does so, no longer by virtue of his rights as proprietor, but in the name of his sovereign authority.[2] Moreover, the motives behind numerous depositions make these political acts of the first order. The king's rights of appointment and deposition thus emanate from his political power.[3]

When abbots wish to retire, they must request authorization from the king to be relieved of their charge. When the monks have a complaint against their abbot, they have recourse to royal authority which can decide in their favor by deposing the abbot.[4] Hereafter, the bishop of the place has lost almost all of his authority with regard to depositions, resignations, and transfers. There is an attempt made to maintain at least his right of approval over the nominations as prescribed in Canon 17 of the Synod of Frankfort, held in 794: *"ut abba in congregatione non elegatur, ubi iussio regis fuerit, nisi per consensum episcopi loci illius."*[5]

The result of this usurpation of abbeys by the king was the frequent change of abbots. Just as the "unfaithful" bishop is deprived of his see, so the abbot sees his abbey taken from him if he

2. Cf. H. Levy-Bruhl, *ib., p.* 170.

3. Cf. H. Levy-Bruhl, *ib.,* p. 138. Nevertheless, the king sometimes deposes an abbot from purely religious motives; for example, Louis the Pious deposes the abbot of Fulda, Radegaire, who was opposed to monastic reform. Cf. *Annal. Laur. Minor. Fuld.* (anno 817); M.G.H., SS. I, 123.

4. In 895, the monks of Corbie depose their abbot Francon; Foulques, the archbishop of Reims, summons them to reinstate him and adds that, if they consider Francon no longer fit to fulfill his charge, they should approach the king and request another abbot. Cf. *Hist. Ecclesiae Remensis;* M.G.H., SS. XIII, 572. The monks of Saint Wandrille obtain from Pepin the deposition of their abbot, Benignus, and his replacement by their candidate Wando. Cf. *Gesta Abb. Fontanellens.,* c. 12; M.G.H., SS., II, 277.

5. M.G.H., *Concilia aevi karolini,* I, 168.

fails in his duties toward his lord and incurs his disfavor. Even if he strives to fulfill his obligations as best he can, he always feels the threat of losing the good graces of his sovereign. It suffices for the latter to balance the services of this abbot with those that he can count on from another one of his faithful, in order for him to judge that it would be more advantageous to have the abbey pass into other hands.[6] The disgrace of a regular abbot often entails the awarding of the abbey to a layman. To provide against arbitrary changes, some regular abbots have their abbeys assigned to them for life; what was once a rule becomes a privilege in the ninth century. Often the evicted abbot's only offense is the possession of an abbey of which the king has need for another. The sudden transfers of favor, so frequent at this time, to which the heads of diverse aristocratic factions were subject, are expressed each time by the acquisition or the loss of abbeys.[7] Therefore, certain ones from among them pass constantly from hand to hand, according

6. Cf. E. Lesne, *Histoire de la propriété ecclésiastique, op. cit.,* II–II, p. 125–129. This is how, at the accession to the throne of Louis the Pious, Adalard, abbot of Corbie, was exiled and deprived of his abbey which will only be returned to him seven years later; Wala, who obtained it after him, lost it in 830 and will never recover it. After the death of Louis the Pious, Bernwicus, abbot of Saint Gall, had declared himself in support of Lothair; Louis the German, having become master of Alemania, established the monk Engilbert as abbot. Eudes, abbot of Ferrières is ousted by Charles the Bald who assigns the abbey to Servat Loup, a religious of the same abbey. Louis the Pious takes the abbey of Saint Calais from Sigismund, who was elected by the monks, and gives it to Aldric of Mans: in 841, he restores it to Sigismund, then gives it to Aldric again.

7. Cf. E. Lesne, *ib.,* II–II, p. 147–149. For example, such was the case of Theodulf who, in 828, was stripped of his abbeys of Fleury and Saint Aignan, as well as of his bishopric. After the conspiracy of 831, Hilduin is likewise deprived of his numerous abbeys and will later recover only a few of them. Helisachar, no doubt on the same occasion, lost his abbeys of Saint Riquier, Jumièges and Saint Aubin. Wissemburg passes from the hands of Grimaldus, arch-chancellor of the kingdom of Louis the German, into those of Ogicius, bishop of Mainz. The secular clerk Alard, abbot of Saint Bertin, is deprived of his benefice after an accusation levelled against him before Charles the Bald. In 828, Counts Matfroi of Orleans and Hugh of Tours see their benefices, shires and abbeys, taken from them after an unsuccessful campaign. It is also the case of the Abbot Hugh, when he loses the favor of Charles the Bald and passes into the service of Lothair II, only to return again to Charles' good graces.

to the whims of the king and at the mercy of his political vicissitudes.[8]

The abbots of the Carolingian period are sometimes monks; more often they are clerics or *canonici,* bishops or simple laymen.[9] From the time of Charles Martel, there were lay abbots by the prince's indulgence, except in Italy; often they even held several monasteries.[10] This secular abbatial charge was most widespread in France. The Merovingian period had already been familiar with this abuse; it now became an institution. Wala writes to Louis the Pious that nearly all the monasteries are directed by laymen who introduce disorder into their communities. This prince himself verifies, at the end of the Council of Aix-la-Chapelle, that most of the monasteries are occupied and ruined by laymen.[11] After the Treaty of Verdun (843) under the last of the Carolingians, the practice of conferring abbeys on laymen again became quite extensive in spite of repeated conciliar resistance. In 909 on the eve of the foundation of Cluny, the Council of Trosly is still complaining about the accumulation of abbeys, the frequent change of abbots, and the number of lay abbots.[12]

8. Cf. Lesne, *ib.,* p. 150. At Saint Bertin, the abbatial charge passes from Alard to Hugh, only to return to Alard; on the death of the latter, Humbrid becomes abbot but remains in office only two years, after which Charles the Bald gives the abbey to Hilduin. In the space of seven years, Sithiu has changed abbots five times. It is the same at Saint Martin of Tours.

9. Cf. Lesne, *ib.,* p. 150.

10. Cf. McLaughlin, "Le très ancien droit monastique de l'Occident," *op. cit.,* p. 49. G. Penco, *Storia del Monachesimo in Italia,* Rome, 1960, p. 367–368.

11. Cf. Mabillon, AA. SS. O.S.B., s. IV, I, p. 494; cf. Lesne, *L'origine des menses dans le temporel des églises et des monastères en France au IXe siècle,* Paris, 1910, p. 70. Louis the Pious no longer wishes to tolerate this state of affairs. Under the direction of Benedict of Aniane, he draws up a list of houses which, in the future, will have a regular abbot. This list has not been preserved; cf. Lesne, "Les ordonnances monastiques de Louis le Pieux" in *Revue d'Histoire de l'Eglise de France,* VI (1920), 328. On the study of Msgr. Lesne, see Ch. De Clercq, "La législation religieuse franque depuis l'avènement de Louis le Pieux jusqu'aux Fausses Décrétales" in *Revue de Droit Canonique,* IV (1954), 392–393.

12. Cf. Ph. Schmitz, *Histoire de l'Ordre de saint Benoit,* Maredsous, 1942–1956, I, 101.

COMMENTARIES ON THE RULE AND HAGIOGRAPHY

Abbatial perpetuity did not in itself pose any difficulty; this is why commentators on the Rule do not linger on the subject. Smaragde says nothing about it in the commentary that he drew up shortly after 817 under the influence of Benedict of Aniane. The teaching of Hildemar, given at the monastery of Civate shortly after 845 and transmitted to us in the double collection of Basil and of Paul the Deacon,[13] simply assumes it:

> Post vero, ordinato capite cum corpore suo, quia non potest aliter fieri ut istud caput, id est abba, non moriatur, ideo nunc de restauratione capitis, id est abbatis, congruo loco hoc capitulum constituit.[14]

In the ninth century, out of eight cases of resignation which I was able to uncover, five are presented as the effect of a desire for a more solitary or eremitical life: these are Bangulf, abbot of Fulda, who resigns in 802 to escape the hatred of his monks;[15] Saint Trasarus, who retires from his abbey of Fontenelle in 816 and, after a voyage to Italy, returns to his monastery in order to lead *"privatamque vitam saecularibus curis exemptam"*;[16] Saint Paschasius Radbertus, who resigns from Corbie to return to his studies and, after the laborious toil of this world, to enjoy the *optabile otium* which is granted to him by God;[17] Rabanus Maurus, who leaves Fulda after two years in office (842) and retires close by the monastery, *"ibique manens ac Deo serviens, coelesti philosophiae*

---

13. Cf. W. Hafner, O.S.B., *Der Basilius-Kommentar zur Regula sancti Benedicti. Ein Breitrag zur Autorenfrage karolingischer Regelkommentare*, Munster, 1959.

14. *Pauli Warnefridi diaconi casinensis In s. Regulam commentarium*, Monte Cassino, 1880, p. 476 (ad cap. 64).

15. Cf. *Dict. d'Histoire et de Géographie ecclésiastique*, art. *Bangulf.*

16. *Gallia Christiana*, Paris, 1571–1650, XI, 172.

17. Cf. Mabillon, AA. SS. O.S.B., (Paris), IV–2, 127; PL 120: 9–24.

vacabat";[18] and Saint Conwoinus (d. 868), who, after the destruction of his monastery by the Normans, lives in solitude, "*In eremi vastitatem redacto . . . solitudinem appetens . . . morabatur.*"[19] Hartmutus, abbot of Saint Gall in 883,[20] Bernard, his successor in 890,[21] and Egil, abbot of Prüm in 860,[22] all of these resigned without our knowing the motives.

Again it is the attraction of solitude which appears in the account of the life of Deols, disciple of Saint Columban. His biographer of the tenth century assures us that, having put his monastery in order, he retired to lead the life of Mary and devote himself to contemplation, after having already led the life of Martha. It can seem paradoxical to say that someone retires from Lure in the seventh century to lead a more solitary life, whereas the same can be highly probable in the Carolingian period. Similarly, when Saint Gregory reports the departure of Saint Benedict from Subiaco, he simply says: "*invidiae locum dedit*";[23] whereas the *Vita et Passio S. Placidi martyris,* interpolated in the ninth century, feels the need to justify this departure by means of a divine revelation.[24] Withdrawal into the desert became one of the themes of hagiography and, thereafter, biographers were fond of justifying a resignation by a supernatural intervention. That adds nothing to the historical worth of the accounts, but it proves that the bond which united the abbot and his monastery had become stronger; to break it, one required a higher motivation. In the sixth and seventh centuries, when the monastic institution was not yet completely organized, the abbot could retire more easily; in the Carolingian period, on the contrary, it no longer depends on him. There must be an exceptionally grave motive and besides this, the authorization of the competent authority.

18. Mabillon, *ib.,* IV–2, 18 and 29.
19. Mabillon, *ib.,* IV–2, 192.
20. Cf. PL 126:989.
21. Cf. *Dict. d'Histoire et de Géographie ecclésiastique,* art. *Bernard.*
22. Cf. Mabillon, AA. SS. O.S.B., *op. cit.,* IV–2, 468.
23. *Dialogues* of Saint Gregory, II, c. 8.
24. Cf. Mabillon, AA. SS. O.S.B. (Solesmes), I, 49.

JURIDICAL DOCUMENTS

It could seem that this marks the end of the principle of lifetime abbots. That is not at all the case. As early as the seventh century, the bishops grant privileges of electoral freedom to the abbeys situated on territory belonging to their diocese. The king, for his part, concedes to his monasteries and to those which have given themselves over to him by way of *traditio* an electoral freedom which is more or less extensive.[25] Under the Carolingians, when most of the abbeys have become royal possessions, they enjoy the right of election as a rule. Under Louis the Pious, the number of privileges granted for free election is considerable. However, it is rarely a question of a free election in the full sense of the word; often the freedom is openly violated, to such an extent that the bishops, assembled for a council in Paris in 847, demand that the conceded immunities be respected. This concession was considered to be a gauge of political order and was granted by a diploma; but it was only valid during the reign of the sovereign from whom it emanated. Moreover, the abbatial election conducted by virtue of a royal diploma only gave to the chosen one a right that was subject to the suspensive condition of ratification by the king.[26]

Now these diplomas of concession of electoral freedom, privileges or charters of immunity, all tended to deliver the abbeys from the control of seculars in order to restore them to regularity by permitting them to have a regular abbot. They contained a formula which explicitly recalls the lifetime character of the abbatial charge. In fact it was clearly stated that the election of a new abbot should only take place on the death of his predecessor:

. . . Et iuxta dispensatione divina cum abba de ipso monasterio a Domino migraverit, quem unanimiter omnis congregatio illa

25. Cf. K. Hallinger, O.S.B., *"Cluniacensis SS. religionis Ordinem elegimus."* "Zur Rechtslage der Anfange des Klosters Hosungen" in *Jahr buch fur das Bistum Mainz,* 1958–1960, 8 Band, p. 224–272. On pages 239–240 and 251–258, the author lists instances of electoral freedom.

26. Cf. H. Levy-Bruhl, *Les élections abbatiales, op. cit.,* p. 153–154.

monachorum ex semetipsis optime regola compertum et vitae
meritis congruentem elegerint, sine premium memorate urbis
episcopus ipse promoveat abbatem.[27]

These formulas are most valuable. First of all, they show us that the
lifetime abbatial charge was generally admitted and that it was
considered to be a right, to the point of being thus represented in the
official diplomas emanating from royalty and from the bishops.
Moreover, they solemnly proclaim the permanence and stability
of this right, in spite of the decadence of the abbatial function and
the transformations which it had to suffer at the hands of kings,
magnates and proprietors. At a time when the abbots are appointed,
displaced and deposed according to the prince's whim, at a moment
when the bishops and proprietors constantly intervene in the
elections and resignations, it is important to see proclaimed the
right of monks to elect their abbot and his right to remain in office
until death, and this in official documents emanating from the
sovereign authority.

THE REFORMS

When Benedict of Aniane undertook his work of reform in
about 785, the abbeys in the Carolingian empire that had a regular
abbot for superior and observed the regular life in conformity with
the Rule of Saint Benedict were rare indeed. Therefore, he endeav-
ored to have this type of observance adopted everywhere and, with
it, the free election of a perpetual abbot. But in fact, the reform of
the various monasteries almost inevitably brought with it, at the
beginning, a change of superior.

It was most often the proprietor who took the initiative of the
reform. To bring it about, it was necessary to place at the head
of the community a man who had preserved intact the cult of
monastic asceticism. Such a man could not be found in the

27. M.G.H., *Legum sectio V, Marculfi formularum I,* I, p. 39–42. In the
appendix to this chapter, there are a certain number of other similar formulas:
it will be seen that this is not a question of an isolated text.

corrupt establishment. The reforms were nearly always accompanied by a change of abbot . . . against the wishes of the monks.[28]

In this state of turmoil and decadence within religious institutions, the councils of the Carolingian period insist chiefly on fidelity to the regular canonical life; indirectly, these decisions reinforce the bonds that unite the abbot with his monastery and his community.[29] His permanence in office is more and more considered to be a duty, an *onus*, and not a right, much less a privilege or simply a provisional charge.

The successors of Louis the Pious, Louis the German and Charles the Bald no longer took account of the promises made nor the exigencies of canonical discipline and began again to distribute the abbeys among seculars and laymen. The bishops, united in council at Yutz near Thionville in 844, rise up against these practices.[30] The following year, the council assembled at Meaux explicitly demands the expulsion of lay abbots. The Church protests against the secularization of ecclesiastical and monastic goods; she requires that the abbatial appointments take place in collaboration with the bishops. But she does not reach the point of complete detachment from secular control; she acknowledges that the king has a certain right of intervention in the appointment of abbots and, consequently, in their displacement.[31]

28. Cf. H. Levy-Bruhl, *Les élections abbatiales, op. cit.*, p. 109. On the contrary, in 848 the Canons of Saint Martial of Limoges request permission of Charles the Bald to transfer to the Benedictine observance. This change was made in spite of the opposition of the bishop, who was won over by gifts, and it was accompanied by a change of abbot. (Chron. S. Martial), *Gallia Christiana*, II, 555.

29. These were, for example, the Councils of Riesbach, Preising and Salzburg (an. 800, can. 2). Some threaten with deposition negligent abbots who do not live according to the Rule, or those who are unworthy; for example, can. 2 of *Capitulare Mantuanum primum*, M.G.H., *Legum sectio* II, I, 195, 5, and can. 11 of the synod *apud Saponarias*, in 859, M.G.H., *ib.*, II, 449, 20.

30. Cf. M.G.H., *Capitul.*, c. 5. This Council acknowledges the king's right to *ordinare abbates*.

31. In his privilege for Saint Riquier, Leo III (d. 816) recognizes this right: "Cum vero abbas loci de hac vita migraverit, nulla potestas nullaque nobilitas

As soon as the papacy has recovered the means of intervening in "Francia," it takes an interest in monastic institutions. It protects the monks against both the proprietors' abuse and the bishops' encroachment. It struggles to emancipate the monasteries from the feudal power which threatened to take away their religious character, and it does not permit monastic life to risk suffocation in an overly strict ecclesiastical organization. To mitigate this double danger, it vigorously enforces monastic immunities and especially the freedom of abbatial election. Therefore, from the second half of the ninth century, the reformers, disappointed in the hopes which they had founded on royalty, turn toward the Apostolic See. Hereafter, the popes intervene, remonstrate with the kings, and condemn the awarding of abbeys to laymen. At Corbie, the privilege issued by Benedict III in 855 includes a direct warning to the king.[32] In 863, Nicholas I solemnly acknowledges the right of the monks to elect one from among themselves as abbot.[33] Belonging to the Roman Church will, in the future, be the best protection for the monasteries. But the struggle will be a long one.

During an early period, the pope limits himself to confirming the electoral privileges which have been granted to the monasteries by some other authority. Then, while continuing its function of confirming authority, the papacy is emboldened and directly grants the electoral privileges to monasteries of diverse juridical conditions who made this request. In a third period, the papacy seeks to hold a special and direct claim on the monasteries which it protects : the right of ownership or of *tuitio*.[34]

mundi in eligendo abbate seu loci procuratione prevaleat, sed in patrum arbitrio consistat ut quemcumque secundum timorem Dei iuxta tramitem regulae S. Benedicti elegerint, hunc, annuente regi Francorum qui tunc fuerit, sortiantur abbatem benedictionem consecrationis impendente episcopo a quo idem electus benedici maluerit." Pflugk-Harttung, *Acta pontificum roman, inedita,* Stuttgart, 1880–1886, II, 27, no. 55.

32. Cf. Mansi, XIV, 118; PL 115:693.
33. Cf. Mansi, XV, 284; PL 119:815.
34. H. Levy-Bruhl, *Les élections abbatiales, op. cit.,* p. 176.

The juridical form of this claim was a kind of attenuated ownership that was designated under the title of papal protection; one of the first examples was that of Vezelay. It is only after the Church will have helped the monks to detach themselves completely from secular control that they will be able to have regular abbots again, elected by them for life.

CONCLUSION OF PART I

It thus appears well established that, from the sixth century when western monachism was organized and the first rules composed, the principle of the lifetime character of the abbatial charge was universally admitted. The popes and councils proclaim or defend it and the juridical documents recognize it, even though it was never made the subject of a formal definition. Besides, such a definition was not necessary to affirm an institution based on the notion of fatherhood; it would not have occurred to anyone that the head of a family could be temporary and even renewable at determined periods. Spiritual fatherhood, as it was conceived by the first monks in the deserts of Egypt, was no less stable. Moreover, it was the ordinary rule for all superiors in the ancient Church.[35]

Canon Law has always preferred the prudence, often paralysing, of full maturity to the sometimes reckless initiatives of youth ; the risks of an immobile government to those of an ambitious one. It ignores the limitations of age and is opposed to voluntary resignations. In a world of slow progress where secular society adopted criteria identical with those of the Church in the selection of leaders, the danger was limited. An optimistic conception of self-development reinforced the position of older men; far from anticipating the evils of declining years, Canon Law presumes the permanence of youthful qualities. The past

35. "The transfer of abbots is contrary to the principles of the ancient law, according to which those who held an office in the Church, bishops, priests and deacons, should not be transferred elsewhere." Gaudemet, *L'Eglise et l'Empire romain,* Paris, 1958, p. 456.

guarantees the present and the future. . . . This confidence explains, to some extent, the dispensations and supports which earmark the clerical structure.[36]

In actual fact, however, how many abbots remained in office for life during this early period? The influences exerted against perpetuity have been seen, some external and others internal. Externally, the bishops, princes and magnates came to dispose of the abbatial charge for their own convenience, without concern for its lifetime character. Internally, many abbots, instead of withstanding an uneven struggle, retired more or less spontaneously. A good number of these undoubtedly sought to recover, in greater solitude and more austere poverty, that monastic life which men and circumstances rendered difficult to achieve, and sometimes even impossible.

Reaction is born from excess of evil. During this period, the greatest disorder reigns in the Church: Rome and the papacy are the sport of different factions of the Roman nobility, many churches are the prey of magnates, the bishoprics have become family property, some are without pastors for long years, and the monasteries are at the mercy of laymen; the Normans who have invaded Europe have plundered the abbeys vacated by the monks. It is at this time, when the royal power is weakened, that the papacy, by vigorous effort, separates Church and State and denies to the king the rights which he enjoyed in the religious sphere in order to take them on itself. Monachism thus regains its independence in relation to secular powers by placing itself directly under the pope's protection. The foundation of Cluny, pontifical property, at the outset of the tenth century, marks a new era in the history of monachism and its institutions. We will see how this affected the perpetuity of abbots.

36. G. Le Bras, *Institutions ecclésiastiques de la Chrétienté médiévale* (*Histoire de l'Eglise,* Fliche and Martin, t. 12), p. 138.

PART TWO

FROM THE TENTH TO THE THIRTEENTH CENTURY

CHAPTER FOUR

CLUNY AND THE CONTEMPORARY REFORMS

THE PRINCES AND MAGNATES had been largely responsible for the decadence of the monastic order and were the most serious obstacle to the practical application of the lifetime character of the abbatial charge; it is also one of them who procured the remedy for the evil. In 909, the council assembled at Trosly near Laon, over which the Archbishop of Reims presided, painted a picture of the situation which grieved the Church and the world; in fifteen chapters it revealed the means for remedying the abuses. Among other things, it determined that "before all else, it was important to return to the regular nomination of abbots and abbesses."[1] The same year, William, Duke of Aquitaine and Count of Auvergne, founded the monastery of Cluny and chose the monk Berno as its first abbot. In order to assure the future of this foundation and preserve its strictly religious character, William offered it to Saint Peter. The new monastery thus became the property of the pope and came under his protection. Amid the general decadence, there will now be a place where the secular hold on religious institutions will be broken, and where the monastic life will rediscover its normal growth in complete independence guaranteed and protected by the Apostolic See.

In conformity with the ancient system, the first abbot Berno had been appointed by the founder; he also remained abbot of Baume and of Gigny, and in 920 became abbot of Souvigny. However, the

1. Mansi, XVIII, 263.

E

charter of foundation granted to the monks the right to elect the abbot of their choice on Berno's death. William also renounced intervention in the government of the abbey by exempting it, in the temporal order, from all alien power, and by establishing a permanent relationship with the Apostolic See. The exemption in the spiritual order was more tedious and more difficult to obtain.

The first case of exemption, that is, removal of a monastery from all ecclesiastical jurisdiction other than that of the pope, is that of Bobbio by Pope Honorius I in 628. It was followed by a dozen others in the course of the eighth and ninth centuries. But it is in the tenth century that exemption from the bishop's jurisdiction would become extensive. Things began to happen at the Council of Saint Basle of Verzy in 991, on the occasion of the strife between Abbo of Fleury and the Bishop of Orleans; the former having prevailed, he obtained the exemption in question from the papacy in 997. It remained to grant the privilege to other monasteries and to broaden its terms to include exemption from the power of Orders. It is the monks of Cluny who obtained from Gregory V, in 998 or 999, a privilege which freed them in regard to the power of Orders by permitting them to address the prelate of their choice for ordinations, abbatial blessings, and the consecration of churches. In 1016, Pope Benedict VIII sends an injunction to the bishops of Burgundy, Aquitaine and Provence to defend the monks of Cluny against all the evils which they had to suffer. He insists on the temporal dependence, relative to the Holy See, of Cluny and of all the places which belong to it; without yet reaching the point of spiritual exemption, he enjoins the bishops to excommunicate those who attack the monks. In 1024, John XIX renews the privilege of Gregory V, which guards the monks from episcopal coercion, and extends it to all the monks of Cluny *ubicumque positi*, thus in all the daughter houses and even those travelling abroad. The development of the exemption as realized here led directly to monastic centralization and to the organization of an order. In 1027, at the Council of Rome, John XIX takes on the defense of Cluny, *nostrum monasterium singulare*, by declaring that it is a member of the one body of which the Roman Church is the head, having a primacy over all the other churches. This success heralded the Gregorian Reform and sanctioned the existence of a new monastic hierarchy. The ancient structure of independent monasteries subject to the bishop was succeeded by that of exempt monasteries, all dependent on the pope. The autonomous monastery is replaced by the affiliated monastery for whom the *ordo*, that is a common observance, is essential.[2]

The reform of Cluny also coincided with a general investigation of the unity of observance. Historians have made note of it: the ground-work of the customs is the same in Lorraine, in Flanders, at Liège, in Burgundy, with Dunstan of Canterbury, Oswald of Worcester and Ethelwald of Winchester.[3] However, there is a difference between the unity realized in a centralized group like Cluny, and that of federated monasteries where each kept its independence and, consequently, a certain number of its own proper customs and, above all, had its own abbot. Cluny did indeed have affiliated abbeys, but only a small number of them;[4] if their abbot was elected for life by the community, the election had to be approved and confirmed by the abbot of Cluny. Moreover, from the end of the eleventh century, the popes never cease to encourage the tendency toward centralization. This is why Urban II confirms the right claimed by Saint Hugh to appoint the abbot of Saint Martial of Limoges. A Bull from the same Pope in 1099 attaches the abbey of Saint Bertin to Cluny and grants to the abbot of Cluny the power to name, in most cases, the abbot of the newly affiliated monastery, and even to depose him if he judges it to be necessary.[5] Affiliation, then, tended toward dependence.

This latter was the regime of innumerable Cluniac priories. The

2. Cf. Lemarignier, "Structures monastiques et structures politiques," *Il monachesimo nell'alto medievo e la formazione della civilta occidentale*, Spoleto, 1957, p. 382–400; and A. Dumas, *L'affranchissement des monastères* (*Histoire de l'Eglise*, Fliche and Martin, t. 7), p. 356–364.

3. Cf. U. Berlière, *Les élections abbatiales au moyen âge, op. cit.*, p. 131; and Knowls, *The Monastic Order in England*, Cambridge, 1950, p. 31–83.

4. A Bull from Gregory VI enumerates nine; another from Gelasius II in 1119, fourteen; cf. *Bibliotheca Cluniacensis*, 1828.

5. Cf. A. Fliche, *L'ordre clunisien au temps de s. Hugues* (*Histoire de l'Eglise*, Fliche and Martin, t. 8), p. 437.

priors of these monasteries must never be elected by their monks, under pain of excommunication; chosen by the abbot of Cluny, they were dependent on him either directly or through the agency of another abbot.[6] These priors were revocable and this, along with their appointment by the abbot of Cluny, is one of the characteristics of the Cluniac Order. In fact, they changed frequently, at least in the beginning.[7] In the eleventh century, when there took place great "retributions" of monastic goods usurped during the preceding era, a large number of abbeys were given to the Order by noblemen; Cluny reduced them to the condition of priories as soon as possible, in spite of a certain resistance which was occasionally legitimate.[8] Nevertheless, while maintaining this principle of removability, the abbots of Cluny and the general chapters were not slow to realize that too great an instability had its drawbacks. Hugh V (d. 1207) declared that the priors should not be changed except in the case of a grave fault.[9] Henry I (1308–1319) again insists:

6. Cf. G. de Valous, *Le monachisme clunisien des origines au XVe siècle,* Ligugé, 1935, I, 187.

7. "Since the foundation of the Cluniac Order, it has been a rule that the abbot of Cluny disposes of his priories as his own property. . . . The abbot of Cluny entrusts the government and keep of his monasteries to those of his monks whom it pleases him to choose . . . and recalls or tranfers the priors thus established by him when he deems it good and useful to do so." Saint Hugh left the prior Gerard at Charité for thirty years, but, in fifteen years, he changed the prior of Sauxillange six times; A. Fliche, *L'Ordre clunisien au temps de saint Hugues, op. cit.,* p. 437. See also the diploma of King Louis VI, cited by de Valous, *Le monachisme clunisien, ib.,* II, 28.

8. "A monastery enters the Cluniac union by subjugation and gift. The principle of the autonomous and independent Benedictine monastery has passed through personal union and ended in a system where one abbey alone, that of Cluny, enjoys not only the fullness of the rights of a regular house, but also a certain number of privileges of domination or supremacy." De Valous, *ib.,* II, 13. There was a transition from the idea of filiation to the principle of vassalage. In the conception of the Cluniac Order, the priors could not be perpetual because they were dependent. The principle of a lifetime superior was thus concentrated in the abbey of Cluny and, to the extent that they were independent, in several affiliated abbeys.

9. *Biblioteca Cluniacensis,* 1366, 1466, 1562. Pope Gregory IX confirmed his decision in the constitution *Behemoth* (1233), no. 8–11: "Caeterum quia

Adhaerentes igitur statutis Apostolicis, inhibimus districtius ne aliquis abbas, prior aut decanus ordinis nostri, priores, et administratores institutes sub eis, contra eorum voluntatem, removeant de locis sibi commissis, sine causa rationabili et justa. Causam autem intelligimus justam, si dilapidatores, inobedientes, aut rebelles, infames, vel alias criminosi existant quibus casibus, si convincti fuerint vel diffamati, se purgare debite non valentes, per eorum superiores poterunt removeri.

The priors then actually became stable and nearly perpetual.

It was by means of the Custom Books that the *ordo cluniacensis* spread throughout the houses dependent on the mother-abbey. Since these have only revocable priors, it can hardly be expected that the Custom Books would speak of the lifetime regime of abbots. The Customs of Ulric (ca. 1083) are silent on the question. Those of Fructuaria, at the beginning of the eleventh century, assume the ancient right without lingering on it.[10] Those of William of Hirsau, in about 1090, simply foresee that, at a time when the abbatial see is vacant, the prior who presides over the election proposes a name on which all agree.[11]

At Cluny itself, because it belonged to the Apostolic See and was exempt, the abbot elected by his monks could no longer be deposed, transferred or promoted except by the pope. The principle of perpetuity was recognized and confirmed. In fact, from 909 to 1400, the abbey had forty-one abbots of whom twenty-three died

---

ex mala ordinatione prioratuum et obedientiarum, et frequenti mutatione priorum multa evenisse detrimenta nascuntur . . . conventuales quoque priores quamdiu in spiritualibus bene administraverint, nonnisi ex certis causis debent amoveri, videlicet si dilapidatores, vel inobedientes, aut rebelles, seu infames, vel incontinentes extiterint. . . ." *Bullarium Romanum* (ed. Mainardi), III–I, 278. Alexander IV and Nicholas IV also confirmed these decisions. *Bibl. Cluniac.*, 124, 152.

10. "Ut exempli causa, utamur electione domni Wiberti abbatis, qui modo est: defuncto domno Alberto abbate, priusquam corpus eius sepulture traderetur, venimus in capitulum . . .; electio domni Wiberti abbatis, hoc modo . . ." Albers, *Consuetudines monasticae,* Monte Cassino, 1907, IV, 125.

11. Cf. *Consuetudines Hirsau,* I. II, c. I; PL 150:1037. They dwell on the procedure to be followed in the case of the deposition of a dependent abbot; *b.,* 1050.

in office, eleven resigned, and seven were promoted to the episcopate or cardinalate. The first three appointed their successor who
was approved and proclaimed by the community. Eventually, an
election was held by mutual consent. The abbot chose three
dignitaries who were charged with the duty of electing his successor
after his death. Later on, even these *fratres spirituales* were elected by
the whole community.[12] The abbots who retired did so for reasons
which do not impair the lifetime character of the charge.

The constitution of the new religious organism presented notable
advantages for the communities and for individuals. The unity of
customs which constituted the *ordo cluniacensis,* taken in its original
sense, was a pledge of good monastic observance; the government
of the abbot of Cluny, extending to all the houses, permitted the
realization of mutual aid and a common defense against obstacles
and difficulties which affected the whole body. By reason of their
union among themselves and their subordination to the abbot of
Cluny, the communities of the different monasteries enjoyed a
greater security, and their spiritual and material interests were
better preserved and assured. But these advantages were paid for in
the loss of autonomy for the monasteries. Hereafter, except for the
mother-abbey and several affiliated monasteries, there were no
longer any superiors elected by their community for life. They were
appointed by the abbot of Cluny and were no more than simple
officers whom he used to further the best interests of the Order.

The initiative of William of Aquitaine was not an isolated case,
and the reform was not limited to Cluny. History has preserved
other examples.[13] The same spirit animated Gerard of Brogne in
the dioceses of Liege and Reims. The abbey of Gorze in Lorraine,
that of Saint Maximin at Trèves, and others became centers of the
regular life due to a return to better traditions. However, they had
another characteristic trait: the abbeys remained independent

12. Cf. *Consuetudines Udalric.,* 1, III, c. I; PL 149:683.

13. Cf. G. Schnuerer, *L'Eglise et la civilisation au moyen âge,* Paris, 1933-
1948, II, 265-268; Ph. Schmitz, *Histoire de l'Ordre de saint Benoit, op. cit.,* I,
148-191 and A. Dumas, *L'affranchissement des monastères* (*Histoire de l'Eglise,*
Fliche and Martin, t. 7), *op. cit.,* p. 343-348.

among themselves and continued under the jurisdiction of the diocesan bishops, except for a few rare exceptions. It is at this time that William of Volpiano laid down, as a condition of his reform, the concession of a privilege of exemption similar to that of Cluny for the principal monasteries which he controlled. The abbeys formed groups among themselves in order to maintain the same spirit and adopt common usages.[14] The reform movement developed under different forms, but nearly always stemming from the principle of a regular superior. Out of zeal for the cause of monastic discipline, the lord proprietor resigned his *abbatia* and surrendered it to the community, to a regular abbot, to the reformer whom he summoned, to the monks of Cluny, or to another reformed abbey. Hugh Capet resigns the abbatial see of Saint Germain in favor of Gualon; at Saint Riquier, he hands over the abbatial charge to a monk from Corbie; similarly at Saint Denis, he restores it to regular abbots. Arnoul of Flanders ceases to be the abbot of Saint Bertin, Saint Bavo, Saint Pierre-au-Mont-Blandin, Saint Vaast and Saint Amand from the day when he determines the reform of these monasteries.[15] This return to regular observance restores the practical application of abbatial perpetuity.

From the second half of the eleventh century, at the moment of Cluny's greatest vigor, a certain number of souls, smitten with notions of solitude and penance, sought to realize, outside of the great order, this renewed search for personal perfection which then stimulated the desires of the entire Church. Hence, there arose various attempts at new forms of religious life.[16] The first in chronological order is that of Camaldoli. It is reported that, in the eleventh century, Otto III, hearing talk of Romuald, obliged him to become an abbot; but the latter, exposed to all sorts of difficulties

14. At Gorze, the monasteries were grouped into a federation. There were no general chapters before the twelfth century. The monks were connected with *potestas exteriores*—bishops or princes—; when there was some business to be settled, they had recourse to the bishop or the emperor who held a *potestas ordinaria* over the monastery and could depose the abbot.

15. Cf. Lesne, *Histoire de la propriété ecclésiastique, op. cit.,* II–III, 20–22.

16. Concerning these new foundations, cf. Mahn, *L'ordre cistercien et son gouvernement des origines au milieu du XIIIe siècle,* Paris, 1945, p. 27–35.

on the part of his community, and desiring to lead a more humble
life, retired "for fear of being the abbot of bodies rather than of
souls."[17] Going a step further, he obtained an abbatial deposition
from the emperor.[18] The initiative of the Camaldolese aimed less at
wrenching monachism from the control of secular power than at
restoring it to its primitive humility and poverty.

Later, Saint Peter Damian, although he did not instigate any
reforms, wrote a treatise *De fuga dignitatum ecclesiasticarum*, addressed
to an abbot who had resigned, in order to congratulate and encourage him. It is a work adapted to a given circumstance and destined
for a particular individual, in which there is question of a sad
condition of monastic discipline and wretched abbots, no less than
uncontrollable monks.[19] It is an indictment against worldly abbots,
great lords who are proud, pompous, gluttonous, greedy for the
goods of this world, and against disobedient monks who are
quarrelsome and critical of their abbot. Under these conditions, in
the face of the dangers of the abbatial charge as it then exists, and
the added difficulties of governing a community which no longer
has a feeling for the monastic life, it is better for the superior to
retire and think of nothing but his own salvation.[20] This could be
considered as a paraphrase of Saint Gregory's text which tells of
Saint Benedict's departure from the community where certain
parties had wanted to poison him. Such a text only serves to
confirm what is already known to be the state of a certain number
of monasteries at this time, but it in no way prejudges the worth of
the juridical bond, well recognized in this period, that unites the
abbot with his community and that can only be severed by the

17. Cf. J. Leclercq, O.S.B., *Saint Pierre Damien, ermite et homme d'Eglise*,
Rome, 1960, p. 26 and 35.

18. Cf. J. Leclercq, *ib.*, p. 32.

19. "Gratias refero, qui te per suum Spiritum docuit, periculoso hoc
tempore aridam virgam vanae praelationis abjicere . . . quis potest hoc ferreo
saeculo monasterium sine sui capitis periculo regere?" PL 145:455. This is
Tract 21 of the works of the saint.

20. "Quapropter, dilectissime, satis laudabiliter et prudenter egisti, videlicet
ut infecundi laboris gravissimum pondus abjiceres, et levigatis cervicibus ad
fructuosae quietis otium convolares." *ib.*, 461.

intervention of a competent authority. In addition—and this is important for the particular age—it is interesting to note this allusion to the spiritual values of the monastic life, at once so vehement and so sincere. This treatise does not constitute an argument against the lifetime abbatial regime, it merely recalls that what counts, before everything else, is the search for God, the salvation of souls, and personal sanctification by means of the monastic observances. Peter Damian speaks out against the manner of life of contemporary abbeys. The juridical framework interests him less than the moral reform. He has also written a poem, *De abbatum miseria,* in which he deplores the decadence of monastic life.[21] The abbots are no longer monks, so involved, so over-whelmed are they by anxiety over secular affairs; in their monasteries, they are the slaves of their monks.[22] It is merely a versification of the same ideas that appear in the treatise. The conclusion is identical: in the face of such a situation, it is better for the abbot to retire and become a hermit:

> His honoribus, abbates venerandi, cedite;
> grave pondus et inane ultro jam objicite,
> et de cetero quieti ac securi vivite.

The Order of Vallombrosa, approved by Victor II in 1055, resembled that of Cluny: the abbot was the perpetual general of the whole Order. As of 1115, Paschal II asserted that he would be elected by the superiors of all the monasteries; if he was already an abbot, he should quit his abbey to take on the government of the one at Vallombrosa. He had ordinary jurisdiction over all the houses and all the monks of the Order. According to Tamburini, the abbot general was perpetual until the time of Innocent VIII (1484–1492) who grouped the monasteries into a congregation.[23]

21. PL 145:972–974.

22. "Si velit de immundo quidquam loqui vitio, monachorum intestina oritur seditio, et occulte statim eius tractatur perditio." *ib., 973.*

23. Cf. Tamburini, *De jure abbatum et aliorum praelatorum,* Lyons, 1650, I, 106.

In 1074, Stephen of Muret founded Grandmont in solitude and poverty. We know almost nothing about its early organization, especially where the superior's term of office is concerned. He bore the name of Prior; he was elected by six clerical religious and six lay brothers, themselves elected. He could be deposed and expelled by the brothers. It was forbidden to give him the name of "abbot."[24]

In 1084, Saint Bruno founded the Grande Chartreuse; but the new Order only became organized a little later when the Statutes were drawn up in about 1130. This will be discussed farther on.

In 1101, Robert of Arbrissel established Fontevrault, preaching flight from the world, penance and poverty. There is little information available on the organization of this new institution.

Bernard of Tiron, first a monk at Saint Cyprian of Poitiers, became prior of Saint Savin, then abbot of Saint Cyprian in 1100. He obtained the permission of Urban II to exchange his abbatial functions for those of an itinerant preacher. Having become a hermit, he finally founded a Benedictine monastery at Tiron in solitude and poverty.

The Cluniac Reform and those which drew inspiration from similar principles had, as object, the deliverance of the monasteries from the control of laymen and the restoration of monastic life to its essential elements; but that brought with it many other consequences. The union of dependent priories with the mother-abbey led to the constitution of the first religious order. For local and familial institutions such as monasteries, this poses the question of relations among themselves and with a central organism or a superior authority: it was necessary to define the powers and responsibilities of this authority. It was at first a simple personal union, which then tended to become a homogeneous juridical system where the various particular institutions lost a part of their rights and their authority in favor of the central organism.[25] For the

24. PL 204:1160–1162.

25. At the death of Saint Odilo (1049), "the Order of Cluny has achieved its period of formation. The principle of the autonomous and independent Benedictine monastery has passed through personal union and ended in a system where one abbey alone, that of Cluny, enjoys not only the fullness of

crisis of authority which is the great problem of the tenth century, Cluny and its imitators offered the solution of a strongly centralized organization with a head who rules over the local particularisms and powers. The superposition, in all spheres, of uncoordinated jurisdictions and powers which are in opposition to one another gives way to a union with a strong hierarchy and an uncontested central power. In a fragmented Church where pontifical authority exerts itself only with great difficulty, Cluny has become the first leaven of unity by establishing the first centralized religious order dependent on the Apostolic See. As long as the monasteries had depended on the diocesan bishops, the possibility of grouping them into a single organism under one central authority was beyond imagining. Exemption was necessary. From the day when Cluny, after its donation to Saint Peter, exempted itself from the jurisdiction of the head of the diocese in order to be immediately dependent on the pope, it became possible and altogether natural to unite houses which, by their attachment to the great abbey, enjoyed the same privileges and observed the same usages.

---

the rights attributed by Saint Benedict to any regular house, but also a certain number of privileges of domination or supremacy over a whole series of monasteries of a different nature. The individual rights of these latter are more or less diminished. All the monasteries participate in the life of one body, of which Cluny is at once the head and the heart; they are but an emanation without true autonomous existence." G. de Valous, *Le monachisme clunisien, op. cit.,* p. 13.

CHAPTER FIVE

CÎTEAUX

CÎTEAUX IS BORN of a reaction against the monastic observance of the feudal age and against the customs which were its mode of expression; it marks a return to the strict practice of the Rule of Saint Benedict. The first Cistercians sought to live, as far as possible, in conformity with this Rule, especially where poverty and separation from the world were concerned.[1] They could hardly help being struck by the differences which existed between the abbot as conceived in the Rule and what he had now become, even after the reforms which had restored to the organization of monastic life its regular character. At Cluny in particular, the abbot, spiritual father of his monks, had become also the head of an order, a great ecclesiastical personage, and even a temporal power; in the dependent houses, there were no longer any abbots at all.

In delivering monachism from the control of laymen, the great abbey still had not reached the point of removing it from all temporal servitude: wealth, power, business worries, bargaining with magnates, the Church and the world. Cîteaux reacted against the whole of such a situation.

Each Cistercian monastery has its abbot who leads the life of the monks and, at least during the first century of its history, is no

---

1. Cf. P. Salmon, "L'ascèse monastique et les origines de Cîteaux" in *Mélanges saint Bernard* (Twenty-first Congress of the Burgundian Association of Scholarly Societies, eighth centenary of the death of Saint Bernard), Dijon, 1954, p. 268–283.

longer the high lord and prelate of previous times. To guarantee the efficacy and duration of this return to sound monastic traditions, there were created among the abbeys certain bonds in accordance with filial relationships. The abbots of the first "daughters" of Cîteaux came each year, spontaneously at first, to visit the abbey that had founded them and where their monks had received their monastic formation: this was the first basic outline of the general chapters. The bonds of mutual relation among the various monasteries were then established and fixed by the *Carta Caritatis* approved, it seems, by Calixtus II in 1119. This text instituted, besides the general chapters,[2] another means of maintaining the union among the monasteries and especially the exact observance in each of them: regular visitations. Historians have uncovered various stages or wordings of this text: that of 1119 called *Carta Caritatis Prior*; that of 1123–1124 known as *Summa Cartae Caritatis;* and lastly a revision between 1134 and 1153 which gives the definitive text, the *Carta Caritatis Posterior.*

None of these texts explicitly mentions the lifetime character of the abbatial charge; nevertheless, they all presume and refer to it in determining the instances of cession, their motives, and the procedure to be followed. It is easy to conclude that, save for deposition or voluntary resignation, the abbot remained in office for life. Cîteaux even offers the first attempt at organizing the institution of perpetual abbots.

The *Carta Caritatis Prior* already speaks of the deposition of abbots who disregard the Rule of the Order, or who make themselves accessories to the vices of their monks.[3] The abbot of Cîteaux

---

2. The Church and the religious orders exerted a primordial influence on the organization of elective and deliberative techniques. It is sufficient to compare the technique of a Cistercian chapter in the twelfth century with the customs and procedures of a popular assembly in an Italian commune during the same period to realize the considerable lead that the Church had in this realm.

3. *Carta caritatis prior,* IX: "24 b. Quod si aliquis abbatum contemptor s. regule vel nostri ordinis aut fratrum commissorum vitiis consentiens repertus fuerit, abbas novi monasterii per se vel per priorem sui cenobii aut per litteras eandem personam ad *emendationem ammonere* quater studeat. 24 c. Quod si contempserit, tunc abbas majoris ecclesiae errorem ejus episcopo, in

should first of all intervene to try to remedy the situation. If he does
not succeed, he should have recourse to the diocesan bishop. This
latter will investigate the affair with the abbot of Cîteaux and with
his clerics. The case could end with the correction of the guilty
party or with his deposition. But it is necessary to anticipate all
eventualities: if the bishop does not wish to intervene, through
misunderstanding of the gravity of the situation or through neglect,
the abbot of Cîteaux will bring the matter before an assembly of
several abbots of the Order, over which he himself will preside;
they will go to the premises in question and, if necessary, will
themselves depose the guilty abbot. Then, in their presence and
with their counsel, the election of a successor will take place. If they
are ill-received by the imputed abbot and by the community, they
will excommunicate them.

In this very precise and detailed procedure, the entire initiative
and the last word belong to the abbot of Cîteaux. In the end, the
deposition of an abbot depends mainly on him. The legislator has
foreseen, as counterpart to this authority, and as pledge of the
exercise of this responsibility, the possibility of the intervention of
the bishop with his clergy and, in the second instance, the participation of a group of abbots. It is true that these latter were chosen by
the abbot of Cîteaux, but their number was a guaranty of justice and
prudence in the decision to be taken. If it is a question of the abbot of
Cîteaux himself, the Charter of Charity anticipates that the abbots
of the first three daughter houses, that is the first three Fathers, will
be charged with handling the procedure.

---

cujus diocesi degit, et canonicis ejus ecclesiae propalare curet. Quem ipsi
vocantes causamque ejus cum abbate predicto diligenter discutientes aut illum
emendent aut illum incorrigibilem existentem a pastorali cura removeant.
24 d. Si vero episcopus et clerici prevaricationem s. regule in illo cenobio
parvipendentes eundem abbatem aut corrigere aut deponere noluerint, tunc
novi monasterii abbas et aliqui nostrae congregationis abbates, quos secum
adduxerit, ad cenobium illud venientes transgressorem s. regule ab officio suo
removeant." In no. 5 the text adds that, if necessary, one should have recourse
to excommunication. Cf. J. Turk, "Cistercii Statuta Antiquissima, charta
caritatis prior" in *Analecta S. Ordinis Cisterciensis,* 1945–1948, I, IV, p. 111;
and C. Noschitzka, *Die kirchenrechtliche Stellung des resignierten Regularabtes,*
Rome, 1957, p. 28.

The *Summae Cartae Caritatis* says approximately the same thing.[4] However, the right to intervene no longer belongs to the abbot of Cîteaux; since the monasteries had become more numerous, the charge would have undoubtedly been overly oppressive. The matter should be handled by the father immediate. It is also foreseen that, in the case of the non-intervention of the bishop, the father-abbot could take action against the guilty parties, having summoned only two other abbots in order to reach a definitive decision with them. It seemed unnecessary to assemble a synod of abbots to resolve the matter: two assistants are deemed adequate to advise the father-abbot and, with him, reach a decision.

The *Carta Caritatis Posterior* provides further alterations and a few additions to the two preceding texts. First of all, it considers the case of abbots who wish to resign voluntarily for reasons of incompetence or from weakness;[5] the father-abbot should receive this resignation, assisted by several other abbots, if he judges that there is a reasonable cause and a true need. There is much room left for the valuation and prudence of the father-abbot and his assistants; however, the accent is placed on the importance of the alleged motives, which is a word in favor of the perpetuity of the charge. For depositions, there is no longer any question of having recourse

4. *Summa cartae caritatis,* V: "If someone has shown disdain for the Rule or the Order, or else if he has given proof of idleness or neglect in the charge which has been entrusted to him, and having been warned up to four times by his abbot (acting either on his own accord or through his prior or by letter), he has not wished to correct himself, when the fault of the unruly one will then have been made known to the bishop of the diocese and his clerics, and if these latter have let him go unpunished, perhaps through carelessness, at such a time the abbot will take with him at least two of his co-abbots and, coming to the house of the accused, they will remove the incorrigible abbot from his charge." J. B. Mahn, *L'ordre cistercien et son gouvernement, op. cit.,* p. 134; J. Turk, *ib.,* p. 140; and C. Noschitzka, *ib.,* 21.

5. *Carta caritatis posterior,* V: "Si quis abbas pro inutilitate seu pusillanimitate sua a patre suo abbate domus illius unde sua exivit, postulaverit, ut ab onere abbatiae suae relaxetur, caveat ille, ne facile ei sine causa rationali et multum necessaria adquiescat. Sed et si fuerit tanta necessitas, nihil per se inde faciat, sed convocatis aliquibus abbatibus aliis nostri ordinis eorum consilio agat, quod pariter noverint oportere." J. Turk, *ib.,* p. 134; and C. Noschitzka, *ib.,* 17–19.

to the bishop; only the two abbots are maintained to assist the father-abbot.[6] It is now anticipated that the imputed abbot will be able to retire voluntarily during the course of the inquiry, without awaiting the sentence and the deposition. For the abbot of Cîteaux, it is established that he will first be admonished four times by the first four Fathers; if he does not mend his ways, the general chapter or a reunion of abbots in direct filiation from Cîteaux, with a few others assembled for an extraordinary session, will depose and excommunicate the guilty party, as well as those of his monks who will not submit to the sentence, without any intervention of the bishop.

There exists still another ancient document, the *Instituta Generalis Capituli apud Cistercium*;[7] it supplies other details concerning promotion to the episcopate. There too, the Cistercians took on certain guarantees which witness in favor of abbatial perpetuity. In order to avoid political intrigues, bargaining and schemes which frequently appeared at this time on the occasion of episcopal elections, the *Statuta* forbid the acceptance of any election without the consent of the proper abbot, if it is question of a monk, and of the general chapter.[8] This resolution must have been put into

6. In the Cistercian Order, the bishop very soon found himself excluded from the appointment, the benediction and the deposition of the abbot, after the Holy See's recognition and approval of the powers which had generally been established in each abbey and throughout the whole Order; later the popes went further and granted the Cistercians a great deal of independence in relation to the bishops. Alexander III in 1160 forbids the bishops to intervene in the deposition of an abbot, and in 1165 he declares: "That the elected (abbot), released from all bonds, should not be subject to any archbishop or bishop and that, after having made profession to his ordinary, he should not transgress the constitutions of his Order because of this profession." PL 200: 390; and J. B. Mahn, *L'ordre cistercien et son gouvernement, op. cit.,* p. 73–75 and 88. We also read in the privilege of Villers-en-Brabant, dating from 1193: "Insuper auctoritate apostolica inhibemus ne ullus episcopus . . . de instituendo vel removendo eo qui tempore fuerit contra statuta Cisterciensis ordinis se aliquatenus intromittat." P. de Moreau, *L'abbaye de Villers-en-Brabant au XIIe et XIIIe siècle,* Brussels, 1909, p. 32.

7. Cf. J. Turk, "Instituta Generalis Capituli apud Cistercium" in *Analecta S. Ordinis Cisterciensis,* IV, 16: first draft, before 1152.

8. "Abbas vel monachus nostri ordinis si in episcopum eligitur, numquam consentiat sine assensu abbatis sui et cisterciensis capituli, nisi forte a domno papa cogatur." J. Turk, *ib.,* p. 22.

practice fairly often, for we know that, during the course of the thirteenth century, there were numerous Cistercian bishops.[9] The same document prescribes that these bishops will follow the Cistercian observances regarding food, fasts, the horarium of the Office and clothing, except for a few instances, but these only outside of the monastery. Lastly, it is ordained that retired abbots will reclaim, in their own monastery, the rank of their entrance into the novitiate.

Cistercian legislation did not rest there. Motives for deposition have been anticipated: the acceptance of novices at too early an age, failure to observe the rules concerning the duration of the novitiate, illegal acquisitions, disclosure of secret information, refusal to accept an election to the mother-abbey,[10] the foundation or transfer of a monastery without authorization.[11] It was also specified, with regard to the fate of deposed abbots, that, if the deposition had been motivated by a grave fault, the guilty party was no longer re-eligible for the abbatial charge without the consent of the general chapter.[12] Another case of deposition is that of an abbot who does not attend the general chapter after he has been recalled to the Order and threatened with sanctions.[13]

Soon enough, there was consideration given to the case of sick or infirm abbots who were no longer capable of fulfilling the obligations of their charge. In 1200, the chapter decreed that provision should be made for the succession of the abbot of

9. Cf. R. Oliger, *Les évêques réguliers, op. cit.,* p. 114.

10. In 1245, the general chapter established that abbots who refused their election to the abbatial charge of the motherhouse could not be deposed except by the authority of their father-abbot or of the general chapter. J. M. Canivez, *Statuta capitulorum generalium,* Louvain, 1933, II (291), 1245, 9.

11. Cf. *Nomasticon Cisterciense,* ed. Sejalon, 1892, p. 274–275, 280, 291, 328 and 395.

12. Cf. Canivez, *Statuta capitulorum generalium, op. cit.,* II, 1223, 17; II, 1227, 16.

13. Cf. Canivez, *ib.,* I, 1200, 56; I, 1202, 39. Here are other particular instances of deposition: revolt against the visitation and the visitator, *ib.,* I, 1217, 25 and I, 1217, 79; simultaneous deposition of an unworthy abbot and his Father-abbot who had him elected, *ib.,* I, 1218, 77.

F

Fontevivo *"qui nec venire ad capitulum nec ordinem iam potest observare."*[14] There is no explicit mention of health, but the texts which will follow show that it could not be a question of anything else. In 1202, a general decree is brought forth, at the end of which:

> Abbas de Altofonte et alii abbates qui prae nimia senectute et invaletudine corporis, aut caecitate, non possunt officium suum adimplere, nec venire ad capitulum, cedant.[15]

In 1229, it is the abbot of Altenberg who is invited to resign *"propter imbecillitatem proprii corporis,"* given the fact that this prevents him from fulfilling his duties.[16] In 1274, the general chapter produces a new decree:

> Abbates qui propter infirmitates continuas et incurabiles per biennium remanserint a capitulo generali, praecipitur auctoritate dicti capituli patribus abbatibus ut ipsi, domibus sic destitutis et dispendiis earum, secundum Deum et conscientias suas provideant, aut per amotionem, vel alio modo iusto et debito prout viderint expedire.[17]

In 1277, the abbot of Tintern having been unable to attend the general chapter for reasons of health, the father-abbot is charged to request his resignation if he does not come the following year for the same reason.[18] In 1279, the abbot of Superado, *"qui propter invaletudinem corporis in suscepto nequit regimine ministrare,"* and who has not attended the general chapter for six years, is deposed, *"deponitur in instanti."*[19] If in all of these texts the obligation of assisting at the annual general chapter is strongly urged, it is always in relation to the state of health; this attendance is considered to be a test of the abbot's capability in the exercise of his charge. If the abbot cannot come to Cîteaux because of the state of his health or the infirmities of age, it is estimated that his condition no longer permits him to carry out his duties, and he is immediately compelled

14. Cf. Canivez, *ib.,* I, 1200, 32.   15. Canivez, *ib.,* I, 1202, 39.
16. Canivez, *ib.,* II, 1229, 35.   17. Canivez, *ib.,* III, 1274, 7.
18. Canivez, *ib.,* III, 1277, 43.   19. Canivez, *ib.,* III, 1279, 26.

to retire, without the necessity of undertaking any sort of procedure. This is the first time that juridical texts clearly consider the question of abbatial cession for reasons of health or infirmities springing from old age.

This procedure was so minutely regulated that it was destined to entail abuses. In spite of the precautions taken to avoid excess, especially the intervention of at least two other abbots, there were irregular depositions. Some father-abbots were punished because of a flaw in the deposition of their sons. It even happened that the guilty party obtained pardon if the one who had deposed him had a very bad reputation. According to an ordinance in 1197 which passed into the Institutions of the general chapter (Part VII, ch. IV), the father-abbots should expect to suffer the penalty of retaliation if they acted with brutality or undue haste. To avoid premature depositions, it was decided in 1234 that no sentence of this kind could be issued outside of an assembly of abbots especially convened for this purpose.[20] The position of retired abbots was also made more specific: they would be received into a house of their choice where the abbot would be obliged to take them in. The general chapter of 1255 renewed the previous decisions concerning abbatial resignations. In 1260, a reaction was undertaken against the tendency of certain Father-abbots who too easily obliged their sons to resign. This was futile, for later on, Popes Urban IV and Clement IV had to intervene.[21] At the time of the reform of 1164-1165, to avoid all external interference in this procedure, Alexander III had already forbidden any Cistercian abbot who had been properly

20. Cf. Canivez, *ib.*, II, 1234, 10; II, 1254, 6.

21. Cf. J. B. Mahn, *L'ordre cistercien et son gouvernement, op. cit.*, p. 205, 236-238. In 1264, Urban IV entrusted the charge of the reform of the Cistercian Order to Nicholas, bishop of Troyes, Stephen, abbot of Marmoutier, and Geoffrey of Beaulieu, the Dominican. In his mandate, he indicated, among the chief points to investigate, the abuses of the father-abbots who, without any valid reason, forced other abbots to abdicate. Clement IV sanctioned the reform in his Bull *Parvus fons* (1264), called *Clementine,* where he declares that the father-abbots who have deposed a son in a very hasty and inconsiderate manner will themselves be deposed, and he specifies the procedure to be followed hereafter, enumerating the faults which entail deposition; other cases should be submitted to the judgment of the general chapter.

deposed by the general chapter to have recourse to Rome and an appeal to the pope.[22]

In actual fact, how did this legislation work? We are fairly well informed on the subject, thanks to the *Statuta Capitulorum Generalium Ordinis Cisterciensis ab anno 1116 ad annum 1786*, edited by J. Canivez. According to this publication's general table of contents, there were proceedings for approximately two hundred and sixty depositions during six and a half centuries; but if we take into account the fact that, in the fourteenth and especially the fifteenth centuries, nearly all the abbots were commendators in many areas, this number is distributed over three or four centuries, which makes for an approximate average of one per year. This is sufficient to prove that the texts did not remain a dead letter and that, if the ancient Cistercians had re-established elected and perpetual abbots in each monastery, they also carefully applied the decisions concerning the canonical visitation and the control of the abbots' government and administration.

Some abbots escaped deposition, such as Saint Bernard whose biographer assures us that, in 1116, he was on the verge of being deposed by William of Champeaux because his health did not permit him to carry out his duties; the matter was even taken up by the general chapter.[23] There is also mention of the abbot of Pontigny who, in 1205, barely escaped deposition thanks to the intervention of the Archbishop of Reims.[24]

The *Carta Caritatis Posterior* also anticipated another mode of cession of the abbatial charge: spontaneous resignation. This could only be done with the permission of the father-abbot, to whom prudence was recommended; besides, he should seek out the counsel of other abbots. This was stated with much emphasis in the Bull *Sacrosancta Romana Ecclesia* of Eugene III in 1152.[25] It was recom-

---

22. Bull of July 4, 1169, in Henriquez, *Menologium, Regula, constitutiones et privilegia ordinis cisterciensis*, Anvers, 1630, p. 56; cf. PL 200:592.

23. *Vita s. Bernardi*, I, VII; PL 185:246.

24. Cf. Canivez, *Statuta capitulorum generalium, op. cit.*, I, 1205, 10.

25. "Addistis quoque ad haec, ut si quis abbas pro inutilitate seu pusillanimitate sua se viderit ab abbatiae onere relaxandum, ab abbate illius domus,

mended that these resignations should only be made for just and
reasonable causes. Here are the ones which were advanced in
particular cases:

> non potest ordinem observare; non potest officium suum
> exequi; non praeesse amplius utiliter possit; ad regimen
> monasterii non valens intendere; ad sui monasterii in spiritualibus
> et temporalibus regimen non valens intendere; securitas
> monasterii.

With regard to health, the following reasons are invoked:

> invaletudo; imbecillitas; infirmitas; aegritudo; impotentia
> corporalis; infirmitates continuae, frequentes, permaximae;
> infirmitatis aut imbecillitatis incommoda.[26]

There quickly arose among the abbots an exaggerated tendency
toward resignation; some even abandoned their charge in a scandal-
ous manner. Saint Hildegarde wrote no less than twelve letters to
German abbots to vigorously discourage them from resigning.
Even if they were not all Cistercians, it demonstrates the frequency
of the case. Nor did Saint Bernard favor resignations; he considers
only two hypothetical cessions of the abbatial charge: death and
deposition.[27] Some bishops, on the other hand, drove abbots to
retire: such as Peter of Blois who demanded that his brother
William, an abbot in the same city, renounce his pontifical insignia
which had been conferred on him by the pope, or renounce the

---

de qua sua domus exivit, postulet humiliter relaxari. Qui petitioni eius non
leviter acquiescet nec quidquam inde auctoritate sua efficiet, sed congregatis
aliquantis abbatibus de ordine vestro cum eorum consilio peragat, quod inde
pariter cognoverint adimplendum." Cf. J. Turk, *Cistercii Statuta Antiquissima,
op. cit.,* p. 123; and Noschitzka, *Die kirchenrechtliche Stellung des resignierten
Regularabtes, op. cit.,* p. 28.

26. Cf. Noschitzka, *ib.,* p. 40 sqq.

27. Cf. *De Praecepto et Dispensatione,* 55, ed. Leclercq et al., p. 289 f.;
trans. C. Greenia, *Monastic Obligations and Abbatial Authority: St. Bernard's
Book on Precept and Dispensation* in The Works of Bernard of Clairvaux, vol. 1
(Cistercian Fathers Series 1), p. 145.

government of his abbey.[28] In 1191, the abbots of Armentera and Espina who had resigned against the will of their father-abbot and who refused to return to their monasteries were subjected to correction.[29] The case of the abbot of Acy is more unusual, but it is resolved in a similar fashion:

> De Ugone abbate de Aceio qui in Hungariam profectus est sub spe reversionis, et non est reversus, sed ibi contra prohibitionem et voluntatem abbatis patris abbatiam suam dimisit, praecipitur usque ad Pascha ad earum locum veniat et ibi stet ad voluntatem patris abbatis.[30]

In 1210, the general chapter ordered the abbot of Les Roches, who had resigned without the consent of his father-abbot, to return to his abbey.[31] The same year, when an abbot refused to reassume his functions, the general chapter threatened to suspend him, *a divinis*. In 1220, the general chapter first reinstated an abbot who had resigned, in order to have him judged in the usual way and then deposed if there was reason for it. In 1228, when the chapter had decided to depose an abbot, the latter hastened to resign, which earned him the prohibition against any future promotion to the abbatial office without the approval of the general chapter.[32]

According to the Statutes of the General Chapters edited by Canivez there were approximately one hundred and twenty-five cases of *cessio abbatis* between 1200 and 1437. From the list of Cîteaux' first forty abbots, ten resigned.[33]

Besides deposition, voluntary resignation and death, there is one

28. PL 207:283, *epist*. 90. See P. Salmon, *Etude sur les insignes du Pontife dans le rit romain*, Rome, 1955, p. 60. Letter 93 (PL 207:291-293) congratulates this abbot for having given up his charge into the hands of the pope and having returned his insignia.

29. Cf. Canivez, *Statuta capitulorum generalium, op. cit.*, I, 1191, 4.

30. Canivez, *ib.*, I, 1199, 12.

31. Cf. Canivez, *ib.*, 1210, 37.

32. Cf. also the decree of 1255, Canivez, *ib.*, II, 1255, 3.

33. Cf. Noschitzka, *Die kirchenrechtliche Stellung des resignierten Regularabtes, op. cit.*, p. 28, no. 1.

more way in which the abbatial charge can be interrupted: by
transfer to another abbey. This mode of cession is also strictly
regulated. The transfer of Cistercian abbots was only allowed
within the same filiation, in order to become abbot of the mother-
abbey. Here are the texts:

Nullus abbatiam suam dimittat ut ad aliam nisi de sua derivatione
transferatur. Quod si praesumptum deinceps fuerit, et qui
fecit et qui facere suaserit etiam deponatur.[34]

Item, diffinitionem datam de translatione abbatum, generale
capitulum declarat in hunc modum: quod si filium ad domum
maternam elegi contigerit, pater abbas translationem facere
potest absque capitulo generali.[35]

If the abbot of one monastery was elected to succeed the abbot of
another monastery, the general chapter annulled the election.[36]
However, there were exceptions, as in the case of Geoffrey of
Auxerre who was a monk of Clairvaux in 1140, abbot of Igny in
about 1160, then of Clairvaux in 1162 and was deposed or resigned
voluntarily in 1165 at the request of Alexander III and for political
reasons; then he became abbot of Fossanova to replace Abbot
Gerard who had been elected to Clairvaux, and lastly abbot of
Hautecombe in 1176 where he succeeded Henry who had been
elected abbot of Clairvaux.[37]

Cîteaux thus marks a return to the traditional conception of the
autonomous monastery with the abbot elected for life by the
community. But at the same time, the Cistercians organized a
system of limited dependence in the filiations and of union through-

34. Canivez, *ib.*, I, 1199, 88 and III, 1301, I.

35. Canivez, *ib.*, III, 1363, 5.

36. For example, this was the case of the abbot from the monastery of
Pont (Pontis) who was elected to that of Villers and had accepted; the general
chapter ordered him to return to his own monastery of Pont.

37. Cf. J. Leclercq, "Les écrits de Geoffroy d'Auxerre" in *Revue Bénédictine*,
62 (1952), 274. Out of twenty-two Cistercian abbots of the twelfth and
thirteenth centuries who were transferred, seven were to become abbots of
Cîteaux and seven abbots at Clairvaux.

out the entire Order. The canonical visitations and the general chapters which followed them permit the realization of a certain mutual aid among the monasteries, the assurance of regular observance, and the remedying of abuses and failures which are always possible. This organization, of a federalist type as opposed to the centralization of Cluny, better safeguarded the spiritual and material interests of the community. The problem of the lifetime character of the abbatial charge is thus considered and resolved according to new forms. The abbot is perpetual but, at the same time, he is subject to regular and frequent visitations and he is also responsible before the general chapter. From this fact there arises a fairly precise legislation and a well-established procedure concerning depositions, resignations, and transfers, which permits changes for the welfare of the communities. Perhaps this system involved too great a subordination relative to the father-abbot, but on the whole, it has shown itself to be highly effective and has contributed not a little to the grandeur and fervor of the Cistercians. This organization has served as model for other orders, at least where the visitation and general chapters are concerned, and the Church eventually sanctioned it. It has also proven that it is not the perpetuity of the superior which is harmful, but the absence of a control and appropriate means of remedying the inconveniences which spring from weaknesses, abuses and incompetence.

CHAPTER SIX

THE NEW ORDERS OF THE TWELFTH AND THIRTEENTH CENTURIES

DURING THE AGE OF COMMUNES society gradually moved away from the monasteries which, after having been for centuries the animating centers of all social and economic development, could no longer keep up with the orientations which life now took on and to whose preparation they had greatly contributed, simply because they were so tied up with ancient institutional structures. It is at this time that new institutions arose which, breaking away from feudal organization, assumed freer and more pliant forms, better adapted to the circumstances. A similar phenomenon sprang up in the religious life.

The beginning of the twelfth century marks Cluny's apogee with Peter the Venerable as abbot, and the splendid vigor of Cîteaux shone out in Saint Bernard. And yet there were souls smitten with a religious ideal whose spiritual needs could not be fully satisfied by either of these two types of institution. Till now, attempts had been made to restore the monastic life as codified in the Benedictine Rule, or to adapt it to particular circumstances; it was always a question of monastic reform and, more often than not, Benedictine reform. Now other forms of religious life would be established. In view of an involvement in secular affairs which was considered excessive, and an accumulation of material goods which surpassed the needs of the communities, two currents of thought developed which led to the foundation of new orders: a flowering of the eremitical life and a return to effective poverty. Vallombrosa and

Cîteaux were already completely impregnated with this spirit and had attempted to work it into the ancient monastic institutions by seeking, through a more or less strict union among the houses, to set up guarantees of a serious and profound renewal. The first Order which was to mark a new stage in the history of religious institutions is that of the Carthusians. Although they no longer had abbots, it is important to see how these new institutions conceived and realized the regime of superiors, especially with regard to the duration of the charge. Did they completely and immediately break with the ancient system? Did they exert an influence on the lifetime regime of abbots?

The Canons Regular were born of the Gregorian Reform: some lived in communities more or less dependent on the bishop, others were united into congregations. Among the latter, some were important, grouping together a number of houses: such were those of Saint Rufus, Saint Quentin of Beauvais, Arrouaise, Rottenbuch and Saint Victor. These congregations had constitutions which drew their inspiration most often from the *Carta Caritatis*. The superiors usually bore the title of abbots in France (as was already the custom in certain communities of Canons during the Carolingian Period), priors in Italy, and provosts in Germany. These titles were in most respects interchangeable, and certain pontifical Bulls speak of *abbas vel praepositus*. Later on, there were some priors or provosts who received the privilege of the pontifical insignia. The isolated houses enjoyed no sort of exemption; consequently, their superiors depended entirely on the bishop who was then the uncontested master of depositions and resignations. The houses that were grouped into congregations tended to become independent and exempt; by the same token, they drew nearer to the ancient monasteries and followed their observances, slightly modified. The status of the superiors should be studied for each of these congregations.[1]

Saint Nobert founded the monastery of Prémontré in 1120.

---

1. Cf. C. Dereine, art. "Chanoines," *Dictionnaire d'Histoire et de Géographie ecclésiastique,* 1953, XII, 399–401.

Although the first drafts of the Statutes are lost, it is known that the ideal which was pursued was that of the canon living in community, with certain practices modeled on those of the monastic life. The organization of the Order was for the most part an imitation of Cîteaux, but with a greater autonomy for the monasteries. The Bull of Innocent II in 1131 anticipates, as in the Cistercian practice, the deposition of abbots who would stray from their profession or the customs of the Order.[2] As for the abbot of Prémontré itself, *"si sui ordinis praevaricator exstiterit,"* the same Pope, in 1134, appointed three abbots who were charged with admonishing him and eventually accusing him before the diocesan bishop, who should be the judge.[3] A while later in 1138, the Pontiff again comes back to the question of deposition in order to declare that abbots who are at fault or who will have become useless to the Order should be deposed by a majority of the general chapter.[4] Here, as with the Cistercians, the right of deposition passed progressively from the diocesan bishop to the authorities of the Order. In 1144, Lucius II prescribes that the bishop should be assisted in the procedure by the father-abbot and two other abbots; in 1155, Adrian IV recognizes no one but the general chapter as qualified for processing depositions.[5] Alexander III in 1177 confirms an arrangement which recognizes the power of the Father-abbot, the abbot of Prémontré, and the annual general chapter.[6]

Since the death of Saint Bruno (1101), the Carthusian communi-

2. "Si quis abbatum Ecclesiarum vestrarum, ab ordinis sui proposito, et consuetudine Praemonstratensis monasterii deviaverit. . . ." PL 179:88.

3. Cf. Jaffe, *Regesta pontificum romanorum*, Berlin, 1885–1888, 7652.

4. Cf. PL 179:387.

5. Cf. J. Hourlier, *Le chapitre général jusqu'au moment du Grand Schisme,* Paris, 1936, p. 257; cf. PL 179:881.

6. "Nulla etiam ecclesiarum ei quam genuit, quamlibet terreni commodi exactionem imponat, sed tantum Pater abbas curam de profectu tam filii abbatis, quam fratrum domus illius habeat, et potestatem habeat secundum ordinem corrigendi quae in ea noverit corrigenda . . . Abbas Praemonstratensis Ecclesiae . . . non solum in his ecclesiis quas instituit, sed etiam in omnibus aliis ejusdem ordinis et dignitatem et officium patris obtineat, et ei ab omnibus tam abbatibus quam fratribus debita observantia impendatur." PL 200:1105; Jaffe, *Regesta pontificum romanorum, op. cit.,* 12813.

ties, who had adopted a good number of monastic practices without the abbatial charge, had continued to flourish. Their first Statutes were only drawn up about 1127–1130 by the prior Guigues (1110–1137). These *Consuetudines Guigonis* simply speak of the election of the Carthusian prior by the religious on the occasion of the predecessor's death.[7] The first general chapter held in 1140 declares that the priors, including the prior of the motherhouse, could be deposed by that assembly if, after having been admonished, they do not mend their ways. The *Statuta Antiqua* (1259) states that the priors who will be deemed inefficient by the general chapter will be invited to seek a deposition; if they refuse, procedures will begin immediately for the selection of their replacement.[8] The *Nova Statuta* (1368) prescribes nothing more. Only later in 1509, the *Tertia Compilatio* will furnish an important precision:

De antiqua et approbata Ordinis consuetudine, singuli priores, rectores, priorissae et vicarii monialiam eiusdem Ordinis in singulis capitulis generalibus, misericordiam suam petere tenentur. Quod si non fecerint, nihilominus pro petita habeatur.[9]

In the same text, three cases of prioral cession are foreseen: death, resignation and deposition, as well as the resignation made at the general chapter.[10] In the beginning of the Order, the priors did not explicitly request "mercy," that is their replacement by another, but they could be called upon to do so. Nevertheless, the charters of the general chapters show that the question of the maintenance

7. Cf. PL 153:631f.

8. "Priores quacumque de causa iudicio capituli inutiles reputati, moneantur, ut petant misericordiam. Quod si noluerint, capitulum utilitati domus providere teneatur."

9. *Tertia Compilatio,* part II, c. III, no. 34 and c. XXII, no. 34; in the edition of *Statuta Ordinis Cartus* of 1681, p. 51 and 184.

10. "Cum prior propter infirmitatem, vel senium factus inutilis voluerit super annum habere misericordiam, significet domni Cartusiae, quae authoritate capituli generalis, faciat ei misericordiam, si viderit expedire aut dabit licentiam convocandi duos priores de vicinioribus et discretioribus, qui poterunt ei facere misericordiam, si hoc rationabile esse iudicaverint." *Statuta Ordinis Cartus,* 1681, c. III, no. 38.

or replacement of all the priors is continually posed. When a prior was deposed by the general chapter, his successor was appointed, and not elected by the community. The priors were thus designated or elected for an indefinite period of time which could coincide with their lifespan if they proved satisfactory. They were neither *ad vitam* nor *ad tempus*, but *ad nutum Ordinis*, and the will of the Order was expressed by the general chapter. It was, then, an intermediate regime, but much closer to perpetuity than to the concept of a temporary superior. This ancient legislation remains in force, the priors beg "mercy" at each general chapter and the definitory accepts or refuses after having deliberated on the matter. Between general chapters, the prior general and, in certain cases, the visitators have the power to depose, *si necessitas exigerit*.

Among the Trinitarians, founded in 1198, the minister general was elected for life by the representatives of the provinces at the general chapter. He could be deposed by five subordinate ministers chosen by the general chapter.[11]

In the Order of Saint Dominic, whose first Statutes dating from 1220 were modified and completed in 1241, the Master General was likewise elected for life. He will remain so until 1804; at that time the duration of the generalate will be reduced to six years,[12] later to be fixed at twelve years by Pius IX. The provincials themselves were elected without any time limit; in 1504, Julius II decreed that their term could not exceed four years.[13] Thus the first of the mendicant orders, while demolishing the framework of the ancient monastic institution and organizing a new structure with a view toward preaching and instruction in Christian doctrine, nevertheless kept many of the elements of the monastic life, among others, the *stabilitas in domo* and the perpetuity of superiors. In order to conform to the decisions of the Lateran Council which forbade the foundation of new orders, Dominic and his disciples adopted the Rule of Saint Augustine, that is, the usages of the

11. Cf. Vernet, *Les ordres mendiants,* Paris, 1933, p. 183.

12. Bull *Inter graviores* of Pius VII.

13. Cf. Walz, OP, *Compendium historiae Ordinis Praedicatorum,* Rome, 1948, p. 92, 540 et passim.

Canons Regular which were monastic in many respects. They had undoubtedly recognized that there was, in the ancient system of the stability of religious and superiors, a pledge of continuity and fidelity to the principles of the foundation. In any case, the social influences, the reaction against the feudal system, the emancipation of the commune, and the sense of freedom have not made an impression on the organization of the new order where the duration of the superior's charge is concerned.[14]

But this new Order, as well as that of the Franciscans, and those who would imitate them, posed another problem, that of the distinction between two kinds of superiors: those who had responsibility for the order, as a whole or in part, and those who governed the different houses. The question was not an absolutely new one: Cluny already had priors dependent on the abbot of the great abbey, and Cîteaux had set up a certain dependence of abbots relative to their father-abbots and to the general chapter. The new orders were destined to go much further than this, in accordance with their very constitution. These strongly centralized orders were composed of a multitude of houses, usually modest, which were entirely subject to the supreme authority and, partly, to that of the provincials. It is also necessary to distinguish, on the one hand, the superiors who were responsible for the whole order or at least a province—a fixed intermediate organism enjoying a certain autonomy—and, on the other hand, the superiors who only had authority over their own house. The former were called major superiors, the latter minor or local superiors. Later on, it will be

14. It was otherwise in the organization of the general chapters. This Cistercian creation, extended by the Lateran Council of 1215 to all monastic and canonical orders, consisted merely in assemblies of abbots and priors of independent houses. It was the Friars Preachers in 1228, under the generalate of Jordan of Saxony successor to Saint Dominic, who introduced a representation of the different communities into the annual general chapters. This innovation will then be adopted by the Franciscans (1239-1240) and some Benedictine congregations. This legislation will also influence the development of the representative institution. England set the example toward the end of the thirteenth century, and then it took root in Italy, Spain and elsewhere. Congar, OP, "Quod omnes tangit" in *Revue historique de droit,* 1958, p. 210 s.

precisely stated that the major superiors are those who govern a religious organism *sui iuris*; they are, in non-centralized orders, the abbots of independent monasteries, and in centralized orders, the superiors general and the provincials. The minor superiors are those who govern the dependent houses.

If the effort of Saint Dominic and his disciples had been chiefly directed toward the struggle against heresy and religious ignorance, that of Francis of Assisi was marked by a pursuit of poverty which would permit him to lead a life more consistent with the spirit of the Gospels. Against the dangers of a superficial christianity, in reaction against a worldly spirit and the thirst for wealth and luxury, the Poverello drew the masses toward a purer and deeper christian life. In the first Franciscan brotherhood there were neither priors nor superiors. It was believed that the quest for the evangelical ideal demanded that all mutually serve and obey one another, without the need of any authority or ruling power. Nevertheless, all the brothers were to obey Brother Francis and his successors. This absence of a lower hierarchy ended in 1217 with the institution of provinces, provincials, custodians and guardians. The provincials were appointed by Francis without any time limit determined in advance and could be dismissed by him; the charge could not be considered perpetual because it was specified that the holders of office should withdraw without dispute whenever the order was given.[15] In 1221, Francis abdicated and set up a minister general with absolute power within the limits of the Rule. But it was not until the Rule of 1233, which was carefully reviewed by the canonists of the Roman Curia, that there emerged a clear distinction between the powers of the provincials and those of the general, still without the latter's being diminished. Nevertheless, it was anticipated that the general chapter, composed of provincials and custodians, could depose the general, who was usually perpetual, if it deemed him unfit to fulfill his charge. The provincials remained *ad nutum* of the general.

15. P. Sabatier, *Actus beati Francisci et sociorum ejus* (Collection of studies and documents, t. IV), Paris 1902, c. XVII.

Meanwhile, Brother Elias was elected minister general (1232). An energetic man, he governed the Order in an authoritative and centralizing manner, convening the general chapter only once. On the other hand, his savoir-faire and his enterprising spirit at the time of the construction of the *sacro convento* gave him considerable prestige and authority.[16] He provoked the discontent of the brothers by certain measures of repression and by arranging for extraordinary visitations. The general chapter was convened and came together under the presidency of Gregory IX in 1239: Brother Elias was deposed and the entire system of government was changed. The minister general's power to appoint and dismiss provincials, custodians and guardians was taken away; the former were hereafter to be elected and they, in agreement with the chapter, would appoint the custodians and guardians. The superiority of the chapters over the ministers was proclaimed. The general was obliged to convene the chapter every three years and no longer according to his whim. At the provincial chapters, each house could be represented by a "discreet" elected by it; a "discreet" from the province, elected at the provincial chapter by the "discreets" of the houses, represented his province.[17]

After this reform, the minister general remained perpetual, but on condition that he continued fit for the fulfillment of his charge, which was left to the judgment of the general chapter. It will only be much later, in 1506, that his term of office will be limited to three years, and then extended to six years in 1517.[18] The minister general accused himself before the general chapter of faults which he had committed in his charge and then withdrew. If these faults

16. Some historians of the Order suggest that the ideal of the Benedictine abbot of that time exerted a great influence on him; in fact, he surrounded himself with a certain pageantry and imitated the splendid constructions of the great abbots. Cf. Gratien, *Histoire de la fondation et de l'évolution de l'ordre des Frères Mineurs au XIIIe siècle*, Paris, 1928, p. 143. Concerning this very controversial figure, see Lorenzo di Fonzo, art. "Elie" *Dictionnaire d'Histoire et de Géographie ecclésiastique*.

17. Cf. Gratien, *ib.,* p. 148.

18. Cf. H. Holzapfel, OFM, *Manuale Historiae Ordinis Fratrum Minorum,* Freiburg, 1909, p. 158.

were considered light, he was recalled to state his defense and then withdrew a second time. After which, the chapter deliberated to determine whether he should be simply corrected or deposed; in the first case, he re-entered to accept the penance. The provincials, who were *ad nutum generalis* until 1239, returned to that condition in 1312. It is only in 1405 that Innocent VII fixed their term of office at ten years. Meanwhile, they could be deposed by the general chapter.[19] The custodians were first appointed without a time limit; in 1508, their term became triennial; the guardians *"resignatione non accepta in officio permanere poterunt"*; beginning in 1500, they had to change every two years.[20]

Among the Minors then, the duration of the superior's term of office was slowly limited to a fixed length of time.[21] However, it is important to recognize that the decisions of the chapter of 1239 point to a democratic reaction in the governing principles of the Order; the superiority of the chapters over the ministers was proclaimed and the representation of all houses at the chapter was decided. A sort of parliamentary regime was thus arrived at, where the legislative power resided with the general chapter, and the minister general had no more than an executive power.[22] One could

19. Cf. Holzapfel, *ib.,* p. 169–170.

20. Cf. Vernet, *Les ordres mendiants, op. cit.,* p. 79.

21. Saint Bonaventure (1250–1267) examines the advantages and disadvantages of the perpetual charge of the superior. The frequent change of superiors can be a cause of decadence because the prospect of being discharged in the near future paralyses the efforts of the superiors and because evil-minded religious scheme to have them deposed. On the other hand, the difficulty of encountering in one person all the qualities necessary for a good superior, and the fact that the prelates know they are not irremovable foster their humility; finally, malicious or incompetent superiors are more easily discarded and the hope of seeing them disappear consoles the subjects who must suffer under their leadership. Gratien, *Histoire de la fondation et de l'évolution de l'ordre des Frères Mineurs, op. cit.,* p. 290. It is only slowly and gradually that the provincial's term of office was limited to a fixed length of time.

22. According to M. D. Chenu, *La théologie au XIIe siècle,* Paris, 1957, p. 44; trans. Taylor and Little, *Nature, Man and Society in the Twelfth Century,* Chicago, 1968, p. 37f., 202ff., the new orientations of the religious life would draw it away from monarchical feudalism and pave the way for a return to the

G

believe that the mendicant orders had a decisive role in the alterations of the system of perpetual abbots, all the more so since they
were not always noted for their moderation and did not miss an
opportunity to bring redress to the faults of abbots and prelates;
in fact, they propagated a certain spirit and laid down new principles.

The Carmelites, whose Rule was approved in 1228, had their
perpetual superiors general until 1598. At this time, Clement VIII
reduced their term of office to five years, and Paul V, in 1618, fixed
it at six years. The provincials had no time limit, but were *ad nutum
capituli generalis* or of the General, and the local priors *ad nutum
provincialis* until the general chapter of 1513 which fixed the
provincial's term of office at six years and that of the local superior
at two years.[23]

The Servites, approved in 1249, seem to have followed the
Carthusian practice. The *Constitutio de modo capitulum generale
celebrandi,* which dates from 1256, foresees that the general will be
able to resign and that the annual general chapter will have the
power to excuse him from his charge. Besides, at each chapter, all
the superiors, including the general, were expected to offer their
resignation into the hands of four *patres prudentiores* elected for this
purpose each year, and whose duty it was to accept or refuse these
renunciations.[24] However, the *Constitutiones antiquae* only speak of
the resignation of provincials and local priors at the general

---

vita apostolica inspired by the pure spirit of the Gospels. However, democracy
must not be confused with the pure Gospel message, or monastic life with
the feudal system.

23. Cf. *Bullarium Carmelitarum,* Eliseo Monsignano ed. Rome, 1715, and
Joseph Ximenez, Rome, 1768 (vol. II, 294 and 376); and Wessels, *Acta capitulorum generalium Ord. fr. B.M.V. de Monte Carmelo,* Rome, 1912, I, 346–347,
464.

24. "Quod liceat generali praefecto a magistratu se abdicare; et patres
conscripti possint et ipsi eum ab officio absolvere. Quod a patribus conscriptis
eligantur in quolibet capitulo quatuor ex prudentioribus, quibus praefectus
generalis et omnes praesides officia resignare debeant, quorum prudentia
praemium bonis, poena vero malis reddatur." *Monumenta Ordinis Servorum
S. Mariae,* Brussels, 1897, 20.

chapter.[25] Concerning the prior general, it is merely stated: "*Postea ipsi diffinitores corrigant priorem generalem, et socios suos et omnes qui suum fecerunt officium.*" It seems then that he no longer presented his resignation at each chapter.

Till now, there are really no temporary superiors, properly so-called, appointed or elected for a determined period of time. Nevertheless, the principle of the general chapter's superiority over the major superiors has made some headway. The Carthusian practice of leaving the general chapter to judge the duration of the superiors' charge has spread to the new orders. Only the Benedictines, the Cistercians and the Canons Regular have preserved the lifetime abbatial regime. The Silvestrines, approved in 1247 by Innocent IV, are still faithful to it: they elect their prior general at the death of the predecessor. On the other hand, the local priors are no longer elected but appointed by the general at the time of the general chapter.[26]

The Hermits of Saint Augustine are the first to have had temporary major superiors, properly speaking. The first definite information on the subject is found in the Bull of Alexander IV, *Solet annuere,* of July 17, 1255,[27] where it is said, as of something already in practice, that the prior general was elected *de triennio in triennium.* It is difficult to determine whether this practice was only several years old, from the time of the approbation of the definitive

25. *Monumenta O. Servorum B.M.V., ib.,* p. 53.

26. "Generalis prior secundum formam canonicam eligatur. Unde obeunte ipsorum generali priore per presidentes capitulo per scrutinium et disquisitionem voluntatis singulorum duo fratres eligantur per unumquemque conventum, cum quibus usque ad prefixam sibi diem ad eligendum futurum pastorem in monasterios, Benedicti heremi Montis Fani conveniant. . . . Deinde aut per formam scrutinii aut formam compromissi sive si fortasse per inspirationem divinam voluerint concorditer et unanimiter in unam convenire personam. . . ." "Die altesten Statuta monastica der Silvestriner," *Romische Quartalschrift,* 47 (1939), p. 91. It is the prior general who convenes the annual general chapter and appoints the local priors.

27. Cf. Lorenzo da Empoli, *Bullarium O.E.S.A.,* 1628, p. 14–15; *Constitutiones,* year 1290, Venice, 1508, f. 28; Eustasio Esteban, OESA, "De electione Prioris generalis Ordinis (E.S.A.)" in *Analecta Augustiniana,* 2 (1907–1908), p. 158–164.

constitutions at about the end of 1253 or the beginning of 1254, or whether it was previously in effect.[28] In fact, it could go back to the year 1244 when a Bull from Innocent IV extended the authority of the visitator general over all the hermits of Tuscany for three years.[29] One historian of the Order even thinks that the General's charge was annual and that the election had to be renewed at each general chapter.[30] Since the new Order was the result of the union in 1256 of different groups of hermits, mainly in Italy, these hesitations and changes are understandable. There were no actual provincials until the year 1290, and these were elected for one year.

The Celestine Order was the first among the monastic orders to have temporary superiors. The first monastery was founded at Santa Maria del Morrone near Sulmona in 1259 and became attached to the Benedictine observance in 1263. The superior's term of office was fixed at three years for the abbot general as well as for the priors of dependent monasteries.[31] The same principle was observed by the Olivetans. The monastery of Monte Oliveto was founded in 1319; it grouped together a certain number of houses living under the Benedictine Rule, and formed a strongly centralized congregation with an abbot general who had authority over all the monasteries, and with a sovereign general chapter. The abbots were elected for a one year term, then for three, and finally four years.[32]

During the thirteenth century then, there arose a change which was to be at the basis of all subsequent evolution of the regime of the major superiors' term of office in all religious orders. Until the eleventh century, the abbots were responsible before the bishop who held juridsiction over them; they in no way depended on the

28. Cf. Lorenzo da Empoli, *ib.*, p. 12–13.

29. Bull, *Quia salutem potissime,* of May 28, 1244; cf. Arch. Stat. Senen., Diplom. S. Augustini Senen.

30. This refers to the work of Saturnino Lopez, *Organizacion y govierno de los Ermitanos Agustinos de Toscana* (unpubl.). I am grateful to Father Balbino Rano, OSA, for this information.

31. Cf. P. Schmitz, *Histoire de l'ordre de saint Benoit, op. cit.,* III 21; and G. Penco, *Storia del monachesimo in Italia, op. cit.,* p. 305–312.

32. Cf. P. Lugano, "Inizi e primi sviluppi dell-istituzione de Monte Oliveto," *Benedictina,* I (1947), 43–81; and G. Penco, *ib.,* 313–322.

chapter, which was that of their own monastery. The conception of a centralized order such as Cluny brought about the first change. Each monastery was responsible before the entire grouping, before the order of which it was a part and on which it depended; its superior had to share this responsibility and this dependence, even when he was an abbot and elected by his community. It is one thing to have to render an account to one's own religious, and quite another to do so before the representatives of the order convened in the general chapter. Once the abbot's responsibility before the general chapter had been admitted, there remained only one more step to arrive at the notion of deposition by the authority of this same chapter. The regular and frequent chapters led to a new threshold by posing, at each of their meetings, the question of maintaining the superiors in office. The limitation of the superior's term of office to a number of years fixed and determined once for all is the last stage of this evolution. Elsewhere it was originally motivated by particular and accidental circumstances.

The Hermits of Saint Augustine were groups of hermits scattered throughout Italy, mainly in Tuscany. The first bond among them seems to have been the visitator general who was sent by the pope on this temporary and renewable mission. When the Holy See then proceeded to unite them, or at the time that the constitutions were drawn up, it was only natural that inspiration should be drawn from this precedent by adopting a temporary superior for a determined length of time, fixed in advance; this seemed all the more reasonable and prudent since the new Order was rather composite, due to the presence of diverse and more or less incongruous associations of occasionally restless hermits. For their part, the Celestines were in reaction against traditional monastic customs and were strongly influenced by the Spirituals. If Peter of Morrone had left the monastery of Santa Maria de Faifoli, it was partly because of dissatisfaction with the Benedictine observance which was followed there; it is at this time that he became a hermit. Only in 1263, after twenty-five years of searching and experimentation, did he and his disciples become attached to the Benedictine Order. But Peter wanted nothing to do with the abbatial office; he bore the title of *prior* or *rector*. It is only when he was charged with the task of reforming the abbey of Faifoli that he became abbot of this monastery and received the abbatial blessing. Nevertheless, the Constitutions of 1275 still foresaw only priors for all the houses. There was an abbot general in 1288, but he soon retired to become a hermit. Finally, perhaps at the chapter of 1293, it was decided that there should be a triennial abbot general. The reaction of the Celestines was motivated by the sad condition of many monasteries, already heralding the decadence of the fourteenth century; but the notion of a triennial abbatial charge was not immediately arrived at, nor without hesitation. Among the Olivetans, another influence is revealed: that of civic institutions. Blessed Bernard Tolomei, before making his foundation, had held official posts in the Republic of Sienna where he had been gonfalonier of the military and captain of the people. But these charges were annual. It is legitimate to believe that, together with the inconveniences of the lifetime abbatial charge, this was what originally led him to establish annual abbots. This however did not prevent him from holding the office for life when he in turn was elected abbot.

CHAPTER SEVEN

ELABORATION AND APPLICATION OF THE LAW

REFORM MEASURES and categorical assertions on the prerogatives of the Apostolic See: these are the essential elements of what is commonly called the Gregorian Reform. The popes, while formulating decisions which tend to make the life of the Church more consistent with the Christian ideal, never miss an opportunity to exercise an authority which they consider to be universal and unlimited. Their actions are henceforth dominated by a conception of Roman primacy; accordingly, they even intervene in the affairs of non-exempt monasteries.

Here are some examples of papal intervention, where the duration of the abbatial regime is concerned. As early as 1073, Gregory VII writes to the bishop of Chartres, ordering him to restore Isambard as abbot of Saint Laumer and to dismiss the one who had been elected in his place while he was on pilgrimage to Jerusalem.[1] The same year, he advises the monks of a certain abbey of Sainte-Marie that their abbot Benedict, who is sick and infirm, has been invited by him to resign his charge.[2] In 1074, he deposes Alberic, the abbot of Holy Savior in Perugia, and orders the reinstatement of the old abbot.[3] The same year, he enjoins the bishop of Plaisance to replace Rigizonus as abbot of Saint Savin.[4] Likewise in 1074, he

---

1. Cf. Jaffe, 4804; *Epistolae selectae*, M.G.H., t. II, Gregorii VII Registrum, 53.

2. Cf. Jaffe, 4805; Jaffe, *Bibliotheca rer. germanicarum*, II, 51.

3. Cf. Jaffe, 4890.   4. Cf. Jaffe, 4900.

orders that proceedings should begin for the election of an abbot at
Saint Remy of Reims, contrary to the decision taken by Archbishop
Manasses to call upon the abbot of Saint Arnold of Metz to govern
the two monasteries of Reims and Metz.[5] In 1076, he writes to the
monks of Saint Giles to suggest that they proceed to elect an abbot,
although their monastery had been entrusted to Abbot Hugh of
Cluny, for this was only a provisional measure, *ad ponendum
ordinem et religionem*.[6] In 1084, contrary to what he had decided for
Saint Remy of Reims, he prescribes that, at the death of one of the
two abbots of Figeac and Conques, the survivor will become abbot
of the two monasteries.[7]

In 1111, Paschal II informs Bruno that he cannot be simultan-
eously bishop of Segni and abbot of Monte Cassino and, consequently, that he should resign this latter charge.[8] In 1112 (?), he
writes to the archbishop of Tours and the bishops of Rennes and
Mans to ask them to espouse the cause of the abbot of Saint Aubin
of Angers, who has been deposed by Bishop Rainaud.[9] In 1114 (?),
he enjoins the bishop of Coire to replace an abbot at the head of his
monastery who had been dismissed while he was in Rome.[10] In
1116, he intervenes in the case of the abbot of Saint Rufus, elected
bishop of Barcelona, to release him from his abbatial charge and
order him to accept the episcopate.[11] At an uncertain date, he writes
to Conrad, archbishop of Salzburg, to inquire whether Pavo, abbot
of Saint Emmeran, has been deposed canonically; after the inquiry,
he orders the bishop to reinstate the abbot and threatens to bar him
from every episcopal office should he refuse.[12]

Honorius II in 1126 hurls a sentence of deposition against Abbot
Oderisius of Monte Cassino.[13] Innocent II in 1135 orders the

5. Cf. Jaffe, 4829.   6. Cf. Jaffe, 5016.   7. Cf. Jaffe, 5267.

8. Cf. Jaffe, 6302, 6303; Petrus diac., *Chronicon Casin.*, IV, 33, PL 164:96.

9. Cf. Jaffe, 6307.   10. Cf. Jaffe, 6488.

11. Cf. Jaffe, 6528; PL 163:405.

12. Cf. Jaffe, 6619–6621. These papal interventions are often exercised
through the intermediary of the diocesan bishop; this is undoubtedly the
case when the monastery is not exempt.

13. Cf. Jaffe, 7249.

archbishop of Trèves to depose Gerard, abbot of Saint Maximin, if the accusations of simony, waste of Church goods and contumacy are accurate.[14] In 1148, Eugene III reproaches the monks of Fulda for having elected as abbot one of their own religious who is deformed and, consequently, cannot be ordained to the priesthood; he annuls the election and obliges them to elect a monk from another monastery, taking counsel with four abbots especially appointed for this purpose.[15] The following year, he writes to the abbot and the monks of Corbie to forbid them to receive into their church the old abbot, Henry, *"quamdiu in suae pravitatis proposito perduraret."*[16]

Anastasius IV orders the monks of Nonantola, on the death of their abbot in 1154, to elect a successor.[17] In 1155, Adrian IV allows the monks of Bonne-Espérance to elect a new abbot on the death of the one who is currently in office.[18] Alexander III exhorts the monks of Saint Augustine of Canterbury to rid themselves of their abbot by having him deposed according to the regular forms, and to elect another.[19] On another occasion, he orders the monks of Saint-Gervais-des-Fossés to choose a candidate from the community of Saint Giles if, at the death of their abbot, they cannot find any qualified person among themselves.[20]

If I have cited so many examples from the eleventh and twelfth centuries, it is to show that the papal interventions occurred in the most diverse cases: deposition, but also reinstatement of abbots unduly deposed; forbidding an abbot elected bishop to retain the government of his abbey, or one already in office to accept another; and, conversely, permission granted to an abbot to succeed another while retaining his first abbey; or simply confirmation of the community's right to elect its abbot on the death of the predecessor. Moreover, these interventions were probably motivated by the recourse of interested parties to the Apostolic See.

In the thirteenth century, from the time of the Decree of Clement IV on August 27, 1265, the papacy established in Avignon began

14. Cf. Jaffe, 7674.   15. Cf. Jaffe, 9231.   16. Cf. Jaffe, 9316.
17. Cf. Jaffe, 9845.   18. Cf. Jaffe, 10093.
19. Cf. Jaffe, 12707; PL 200:1080.   20. Cf. Jaffe, 12759.

to intervene in abbatial appointments, by virtue of the pontifical reserve, for the conferment of benefices whose bearers had died in the Curia, and later on for all kinds of benefices. The interference of the Roman Curia made itself felt more specifically in the instances of contested or double elections. The intervention of the Holy See resulted from the fact that certain individuals had recourse to Rome either to request an abbey, that is to obtain a papal recommendation in view of a coming election, or to gain papal influence on the bishops in support of a given candidate. The pope also had to intervene in cases of legal recourse to his supreme authority: from the thirteenth century on, lawsuits regarding abbatial elections, resignations and depositions were innumerable.[21]

In his Decrees, a great methodical compilation of the sources of Canon Law composed in about 1140, Gratian includes the whole disciplinary tradition of the western Church. It was inevitable that he should come to speak of the duration of the abbatial charge. He does so in treating of resignation. In Part II, Cause XVIII, Question II, the following is put forth: "*An per episcopum abbas sit eligendus et ordinandus, an tantummodo a propriis fratribus sit instituendus*"; he responds by citing the texts of Pelagius I and Saint Gregory the Great, with which we are already familiar. In Chapter V, *De libertate monachorum*, he recalls the ancient principle, universally admitted: "*Defuncto vero abbate cuiusquam congregationis non extraneus eligatur. . . .*"[22] In Canon VIII, Gratian arrives at the question of resignation of the abbatial charge: "*Cum permissione episcopi abbas locum suum deserere potest. Abbas pro humilitate, et cum permissione episcopi locum suum potest relinquere. . . .*"[23] This same Canon recalls the text of Pelagius: "*Unde Pelagius Papa scribit Opilioni defensori*

21. Cf. U. Berlière, *Les élections abbatiales, op. cit.,* p. 53-90.

22. *Corpus Juris Canonici,* ed. Friedberg, II, c. 829, which adds in a note: "Caput hoc habetur in decreto concilii Lateranensis, edito a b. Gregorio proquiete ac libertate monachorum, quod extat in II tomo conciliorum inter decreta Gregorii I, eiusque magnam partem ipsemet refert lib. 7 reg. indict. prima, epist. 18 Mariniano episcopo Ravennati."

23. The ordinary gloss reflects Canon 50 of the Fourth Council of Toledo (633). In fact, this Canon speaks only of clerics who wish to become monks and forbids the bishops to oppose them. But Canon 51 adds that the bishops

dicens: Non licet monachis abbates pro suo arbitrio expellere, aut alios ordinare."[24] Therefore, the duration of the abbatial charge does not depend on the will of the monks; this is repeated in Canon IX:

> Nullam potestatem de cetero, nullam licentiam monachis relinquimus, pro arbitrio suo aut abbates expellere, aut sibimet alios ordinare; quia nulla auctoritas remanebit abbati, si monachorum potestati ceperit subiacere.

The deposition of the abbot is the subject of Canon XV:

> Abbas qui cautus in regimine non fuerit, a proprio episcopo et a vicinis abbatibus a suo arceatur honore. Si quis abbas cautus in regimine, humilis, castus, misericors, discretus, sobriusque non fuerit, ac divina praecepta verbis et exemplis non ostenderit, ab episcopo, in cuius territorio consistit, et a vicinis abbatibus, et ceteris Deum timentibus a suo arceatur honore ; etiam si omnis congregatio vitiis suis consentiens eum abbatem habere voluerit.[25]

Canon XVI again returns to this point, recalling Canon XXI of the First Council of Orleans in 511,[26] and Canon XVII which insists on the dependence of the monks relative to the diocesan bishop.

There, in brief, is the entire ancient law concerning the lifetime character of the abbatial charge, resignations, depositions, and the powers of the bishop.

---

have over the monks only the rights stipulated in the canons: they should exhort them to lead holy lives, install the abbots and other officers, and correct the abbots. Cf. Hefele–Leclercq, III, 273, which refers to Cause XVIII, q. II, c. I.

24. PL 72:748; cf. above, p. 24.

25. The ordinary gloss adds: "Ergo videtur quod aliquis potest deponi propter simplicitatem, ut hic et 74 dist. episcoporum. Sed dicas, quod hic vocat illum incautum, qui negligens est, nam propter negligentiam deponitur aliquis, ut 81 dist. dictum. Vel dic quod abbates propter modicas causas possunt removeri."

26. "In episcoporum potestate abbates consistant. Abbates pro humilitate religionis in episcoporum potestate consistant et si quid extra regulam fecerint, ab episcopo corrigantur"; cf. Maassen, *Concilia aevi merovingici, op. cit.*, 7, and above, p. 12.

The Fourth Lateran Council, held in 1215, legislates on the procedure for the election of the abbot. Till now,

> from the moment that there was agreement (laudatio) on a pro-
> posed candidate, there was a canonical election. If, later on, the
> kings in their privileges of immunity and the popes in their Bulls
> of protection confirm the freedom of election, it is understood
> that this freedom consists essentially in the acceptance of a monk
> from the community, or an outsider proposed or postulated for
> by this community, indicated by the sovereign, the bishop,
> or by a member of the community ; and that this freedom and
> the canonicity of the election are consistent with the episcopal,
> imperial or royal consent and investiture.[27]

Canon XXIV anticipates three forms of election: by ballot, where three scrutators collect the votes secretly and by word of mouth,

---

27. U. Berlière, *Les élections abbatiales, op. cit.,* p. 4. For a long time, the Church was the only institution where the principle of election by the governed was maintained, in conformity with the saying of Saint Leo: "Qui praefuturus est omnibus, ab omnibus eligatur." (PL 54:628). Unfortunately, the mechanics of the elections were often corrupted by interventions from those outside the Church. The election of an abbot was often reduced to the presentation of a name. Even when there was a true election, there was no question of a majority principle. The election really depended on a kind of unanimous impulse toward one person. The unanimous vote was usually preceded by a presentation (*nominatio*) of candidates, followed by a *tractatio* destined to eliminate discord and allow for the arrival at unanimity. From the sixth to the twelfth century, the election of abbots, bishops, and popes was accomplished by unanimity, by personal inclination, or by force. It was not until 1130 that a pope was elected by a majority vote. It is during the course of the thirteenth century that there appears a precise affirmation of the majority principle. The words *majoritas* and *pluralitas* never have their actual meaning; they are not found in any of the ancient religious rules. The principle of a majority is the fruit of a long evolution, tentative and faltering, chiefly among the Italian communes. The Carthusians, in 1256, determined that, for a decision to assume the force of law, it sufficed that it be adopted by a majority of votes. About the same time, under the influence of the communes and the mendicant orders, the practice of the majority principle became generalized. At present, the nostalgia for unanimity is still translated into a recourse to special majorities, for example two thirds of the votes. Cf. L. Moulin, "Les origines religieuses des techniques électorales et délibératives modernes" in *Revue internationale d'Histoire politique et constitutionnelle,* April–June 1953, passim.

write them down and issue the results; by mutual agreement, a method of election in two stages which was the most ordinary one used in the Middle Ages; finally, by acclamation or inspiration.[28] Canon XII prescribes that a general chapter of the various religious orders in the same provinc eshould be held every three years. The subjects to be treated here will be reform, the observance of the Rules, and the election of capable individuals who, in the name of the pope, will visit all the monasteries, according to their fixed duty, to correct and reform whatever admits of the need. It adds that, if they meet with incompetent or blameworthy superiors, the visitators will denounce them before the bishop; if he does not wish to depose them, the cause should be brought before the Holy See.[29]

A little later on, in 1234, one of the Decrees of Gregory IX comes back to the same subject in order to specify the procedure to be followed. If the visitators find a lax and negligent abbot, let them denounce him without delay before the diocesan bishop, and let him appoint a capable coadjutor who will govern the monastery until the next general chapter. If the abbot wastes the goods of the monastery, or if it is necessary to depose him for just reasons, let the bishop, in agreement with the visitators, make him leave, and let him appoint an administrator capable of managing the temporal affairs while awaiting a new election. However, the bishop cannot depose an abbot without the consent of the chapter of his cathedral. The deposition of an exempt abbot is reserved to the Holy See, but while awaiting the sentence, the visitators and presidents of the general chapter can suspend him from the administration of his

---

28. Cf. Hefele-Leclercq, V, 1353.

29. "Ordinentur etiam in eodem capitulo religiosae ac circumspectae personae, quae singulas abbatias ejusdem regni sive provinciae . . . secundum formam sibi praefixam, vice nostra studeant visitare, corrigentes et reformantes quae correctionis et reformationis officio viderint indigere: ita quod si rectorem loci cognoverint ab administratione penitus amovendum, denuncient episcopo proprio, ut illum amovere procuret: quod si non fecerit, ipsi visitatores hoc referant ad apostolicae Sedis examen." This text was inserted in the *Corpus Juris Canonici,* I. III, tit. XXXV, De statu monachorum, c. 7.

monastery and set up a provisional replacement.[30] The Decrees of
Gregory X speak of resignations and specify that they should be
motivated by a just and legitimate cause and, besides, should be free,
without fraud or violence, and accepted by the legitimate authority.[31]

There we have a complete summary of the law at that time
concerning the lifetime regime, the deposition and the resignation of
abbots. How was this law, thus elaborated, put into practice?

It must be noted, first of all, that the Roman Curia hardly
facilitated the application of this law. From the middle of the
thirteenth century, monasteries become an important source of
revenues in the hands of the Curia and of the princes. Abbatial
provisions are taxed at a high price; the priories begin to be the
endowment of cardinals and high prelates, while they await
generous distribution among their protégés. From this arose
multiple interventions in the regime of superiors and constant
attacks on the provided norms. Where the spirit of ambition and
greed dominates, laws count for little.[32]

The strict regulation which we have just seen left untouched the
question of the promotion of abbots. With the Gregorian Reform,
there was an exceptional multiplication of monk-bishops; it
reached such proportions that it provoked a fiery reaction on the

---

30. *Decretales*, l. III, tit. XXXV, c. 7–8. Cf. J. Baucher, art. "Abbés", *Dictionnaire de Droit Canon*, where this text from the Decrees is extensively cited
in the collections of the general chapters of the English monasteries; cf. W.
A. Pantin, "Documents illustrating the Activities of the general and provincial
Chapters of the English black monks, 1215–1540" in *The Royal Historical
Society*, XLV, XLVII, LIV, London, 1931–1937, t. I, 275. The Decrees also
enumerate a certain number of causes motivating deposition: cf. *ib.*, c. 2, 3
and 8; I. II, tit. XXVII, c. 22.

31. Cf. *Decretales*, l. I, tit. IX, c. 10.

32. Cf. U. Berlière, *Le recrutement dans les monastères bénédictins aux XIIIe
and XIVe siècles* (Memoires of the Royal Academy of Belgium, Letters,
XVIII, 1924, no. 1309), p. 4. Nevertheless, there were monasteries which
fought against these excesses. At Cluny, there are no examples of priories in
commendam before the end of the thirteenth century; the case was rare all
during the fourteenth century. Cf. De Valous, *Le monachisme clunisien, op.
cit.*, I, 195.

part of the secular clergy.[33] The case of Abbot Anselm of Bec is interesting. Elected to the Archbishopric of Canterbury against his will, he then makes up his mind to accept in order to obey the will of God. At which time, he addresses a letter to his monks to ask that they not oppose his election; Gondulf bishop of Rochester supports this request. It is also pointed out to them that they will eventually be obliged to yield. A little later on, Saint Anselm thanks the monks of Bec for having given their consent: he has received the announcement from two monks, but he would like to have written confirmation. Besides, this consent was not unanimous. Against his opponents, Anselm justifies his departure.[34] It is interesting to verify, in all of these random texts, the recognition of a juridical bond between the abbot and his community. Saint Anselm calls for a true consent which is only given after deliberation, during which an opposition is manifest, and which must be confirmed in writing. Only after all of this can the abbot resign and leave his abbey. If the monks could not rid themselves of their abbot at will, they could at least prevent him from leaving by virtue of the juridical bond which binds him to his abbey.[35]

The cases of deposition were numerous during this period.[36] The principal causes invoked were the waste of monastery goods, their monopoly or distribution among the families of the abbots, other forms of nepotism, prodigality, lordly ostentation, simony, acts of violence, and debauchery: these are revealed in the pontifical

33. Cf. Oliger, *Les évêques réguliers, op. cit.,* p. 71. The Cistercians and the Canons Regular furnished a considerable number of bishops and cardinals.

34. Cf. Letters 148, 150, 151, 155, 156. S. Schmitt. *S. Anselmi Cantuariensis archiepiscopi Opera omnia,* Seckau-London, 1938–1951, vol. IV, 3–21.

35. Innocent IV still requires the consent of the community for promotions to a bishopric. Once the question is definitely settled by Boniface VIII (1294–1303), the canonists are won over to the position of the Decree, *Si religiosus.* Hereafter, the consent of the candidate's superior is sufficient; cf. Oliger, *Les évêques réguliers, op. cit.,* p. 169, 185.

36. Cf. U. Berlière, *Les élections abbatiales, op. cit.,* p. 71–90: list of depositions in the twelfth and thirteenth centuries. See also G. Schreiber, *Kurie und Kloster im 12 Jahrhundert,* Stuttgart, 1910, 2 vol., I, p. 166–171; the same author speaks of resignations and transfers on pages 147 and 149.

acts and the chronicles of the monasteries. The evil was not universal, but it was profound and extensive. During the thirteenth century, as long as there were on the pontifical throne such energetic men as Innocent III, Honorius III and Gregory IX, the papacy effectively fought against excesses and often deposed abbots. Later, the supernatural spirit was weakened and morals became steeped in materialism. The Holy See itself was the victim of all kinds of temporal difficulties and preoccupations which "push into the background the progressive disintegration of religious discipline in some institutions where virtually the only thing recognized and appreciated is financial worth."[37] The depositions did not always move along without impediments and resistance: the guilty parties found support among the seculars and even with ecclesiastical dignitaries. The depositions took place either after regular canonical or pastoral visitations (this is how Robert Grosseteste, bishop of Lincoln, dismissed seven abbots and four priors in 1236 during the course of his diocesan visitation), or after denunciations and inquiries made at the monasteries to verify given information.[38]

The abbots who depended on the diocesan bishop could not

37. U. Berlière, *ib.,* p. 72; see also p. 89.

38. On the depositions effected by Robert Grosseteste, cf. U. Berlière, *ib.,* 72. The *Liber de rota verae religionis* (beginning of the thirteenth century), attributed to Hugh of Fouilloy (ms. II/1076, of the Royal Library of Belgium, originating from the Cistercian abbey of Aulne, cf. *Saint Bernard et l'art des cisterciens,* Museum of Dijon, 1953, no. 105, pl. VII), represents in fol. 82, around the wheel of true religion, four figures of abbots, each with a legend; the first on the left bears the inscription: "Hic ascendit ad dignitatem sanctam contra propriam voluntatem invitus trahitur"; above, the abbot is seated on a throne, cross in hand, with the inscription: "Abbas hic manet in dignitate sancta cum caritate; nolens dominatur." On the right, the abbot in his cowl, with the words: "Hic deserit dignitatem sanctam propter verbum humilitatis; rogans absolvitur." Below, the abbot seated reads from a book:"Hic sedet in paupertate sancta cum hilaritate; sponte subicitur; sponte subesse volo." See also *Archivum latinitatis Medii Aevi,* 39 (1959) 219–228 and 40 (1960) 15–38. A miniature of the Bible of Saint Omer from the same period was inspired by a similar idea. It represents the wheel of dissimulation, around which are four religious: above, the abbot who *praeest per superbiam;* on the right, the prior *ascendit per pecuniam;* on the left, *supprior nolens deicitur;* finally, below, a prostrate religious represents *abbas dejectus suam dolet confusionem.* Reproduced by C. Poulet, *Histoire du Christianisme,* II, 891.

resign their charge except with his permission; those who were exempt needed the approval of the pope. All were obliged to request authorization to resign; an inquiry was then made to verify the freedom of the resignation and the reasons which motivated it. If it was question of an exempt monastery, the pope appointed a commission.[39] In some cases, the abbots abdicated to spend the rest of their days in retirement and prayer, sometimes even in solitude.

Out of thirty-four cases of resignation which could be uncovered for the period which extends from the tenth to the thirteenth century, sixteen would be motivated, according to the documents, by the love of solitude, a desire for the eremitical life, or a need to facilitate devotion to prayer;[40] six occurred in order to escape the problems of administration or the special difficulties in a given community;[41] five abbots retired for reasons of age or illness, and

39. In 1218, the abbot of Vezelay, broken by illness, resigned in order to live in seclusion; but since he did so without the authorization of the pope, he had to resume his charge. The pontifical commissioners would then see whether there is cause for accepting his resignation and proceeding to a new election. Likewise, in 1244, the abbot of Saint William of the Desert resigned, without permission from the Holy See; he had to be reinstated in his charge and then present his resignation to the pope. At Saint Epvre de Toul in the same year, the abbot, seriously ill, resigned at the instigation of an ambitious monk: the pope annuls the action. At Pulsano, the abbot's resignation had been obtained by force: the pope annuls it, but since the abbot had already retired, he gives him a successor. At Saint Denis in 1238, the inquiry has revealed that the abbot governed his monastery well; the pope then obliges him to remain. Cf. U. Berlière, *Les élections abbatiales, op. cit.*, 65.

40. These are: Blessed Mazelin, abbot of Saint Peter of Salzburg, in 1025; Saint Gurloes, abbot of Quimperley, in 1029; Saint Gerwin, d. 1107; Saint Robert of Molesmes, d. 1110; Blessed Rainald, abbot of Fussenich, d. after 1131; Saint Arnold, abbot of Gemblous, d. 1155; Blessed Serlo, abbot of Savigny, d. 1158; Blessed William of Saint Thierry, d. 1148; Alan of Flanders, abbot of Arivour, d. 1185; Walter of Dickebusch, abbot of Dunes, d. 1189 Ulrich, abbot of Villers, d. 1196; Blessed Joachim, abbot of Flora, d. 1202; Hermann, abbot of Himmerode, d. ca. 1225; Blessed Rodrigues, abbot of Silos, 1242–1276; Arnoul of Louvain, abbot of Villers, d. ca. 1250; Henry II, abbot of Baumgarten and of Holy Cross, d. 1284.

41. These are: Saint Ellinger, abbot of Tegernsee, d. 1056; Saint Adelhelm, abbot of Burgos, d. 1097; Saint Ernest, abbot of Zwiefallen, d. 1148; Blessed Humbert, abbot of Igny, d. 1148; Blessed Geoffrey of Auxerre, d. ca. 1190; Saint Charles, abbot of Villers, d. 1213.

H

seven for unknown reasons. However, it is perhaps best not to attach too great a worth to the formulas employed by hagiographers and biographers. Just as in the eighth and ninth centuries the abbots retired to "become hermits," so in the twelfth and thirteenth century they left the worries of administration to devote themselves to pious works: "*quietem contemplationis desiderans . . . , ipsi soli Deo vacare salutique animarum paterne intendere satagebat. . . .*" It is likewise important to take into account the attraction exercised by the Order of Cîteaux and by Saint Bernard; many quit their charge in order to join him. In addition, during the twelfth and especially the thirteenth century, most resignations entailed the payment of a pension by the community to the old abbot, thus procuring for him a convenient and enviable retreat. This was a supplementary accusation, often added to the prodigality attributed to the resigning abbot.[42] Another consequence of these resignations was that, in the thirteenth century, a law was made of the practice according to which only the pope could legitimately accept the resignation of a major benefice; the abbots who wished to renounce their charge thus had to do so into the hands of the pope or one who had received from him a special mandate. But resignation into the hands of the pope signified that the office was vacant *apud Sedem Apostolicam,* and that only the pope could dispose of it; there need not be any election.[43]

During the twelfth and especially the thirteenth century, there was an abundance of abbatial resignations from those who were

42. Cf. U. Berlière, *Les élections abbatiales, op. cit.,* p. 64–67. Occasionally, to avoid this expense, the resigning abbot is authorized to retire into an *obedience* of the monastery whose income has been appropriated for him, or else to have lodging apart with a servant. In other cases, the old abbot will have to be content with "an ordinary or monachal prebend" and be subject to a new abbot. This is often the case when, to avoid being examined by the visitators, the abbot abdicates of his own accord. At other times, the pope accepts the resignation and decides that, if it is for reasons of health, the abbot cannot remain in the common refectory and dormitory, he will receive a pension, but only with the promise of obedience to the new superior.

43. Cf. *Decretales Gregorii* IX, 1, 9, 9 and 10; ed. Friedberg, 107 s. Cf. J. P. Muller, "Les élections abbatiales sous Clement V," *Studia Benedictina,* 1947 (*Studia Anselmiana,* XVIII–XIX).

weary and incapable of remedying some very grave situation in their monastery. At Aspach, in less than thirty years there are five abbots who resign. At Priefling, there are six from 1232 to 1306. At Reichenbach from 1239 to 1301 nearly all resign. At Saint Jacques de Liège in the thirteenth century, out of eight abbots, four resign. At Liessies, of twelve abbots since 1147, only four die in office; of the other eight, five abdicate and three are deposed. At Saint Trond in the beginning of the thirteenth century, two abbots are deposed and two others resign. In the early days of the Premonstratensian Order, resignations were likewise very frequent.[44]

CONCLUSION OF PART II

The monastic reform, realized in two instances, first at Cluny and then at Cîteaux, restored to the monasteries their independence relative to the secular power and the bishops, and to the abbots the election for life by their monks; at the same time, the new Cistercian Order instituted, under the form of general chapters and regular visitations, efficacious means for maintaining monastic observance and remedying the inconveniences of abbatial perpetuity. The great movement of the twelfth and thirteenth centuries brought forth new conceptions with the foundation of the mendicant orders. A growing centralization, the supreme authority of general chapters, the abbots' responsibility before these latter, and the representation of all the dependent houses in these great assemblies tended to orientate the evolution of forms of religious life even within monastic orders themselves, and in particular, led to the regime of temporary superiors. The ideas of the surrounding world were not ali n o this evolution.

44. Cf. U. Berlière, *Les élections abbatiales, op. cit.,* p. 68–69, which recalls these words of H. Lamy, historian of the Tongerloo abbey: "The greater or lesser frequency of abbatial resignations is one of the signs which, for want of more accurate information, should enter into account when identifying the condition of a community and its leaders. . . . The rapid transition of elected officials, abbots and administrators in the monasteries, especially the heads of orders, was destined to be fatal to the discipline as well as to the finances."

Beginning in tenth century Italy, the assemblies of magnates elect and depose their sovereign. It is in the communes, especially the Italian ones, that are found the first traces of an electoral system, however imperfect. Originally, the duration of the mandate for consuls and counsellors was one year, with re-election prohibited for one, two or even five years. In the twelfth century, the Podesta were even reduced to six months.[45] In reaction against the feudal system, the western world passes into a corporate regime from which issues a municipal current, chiefly in Italy, whereas Germany remains longer attached to the old forms of government. France, on the other hand, tends toward centralization. The Aristotelian idea of the city is transformed in the notion of order or of an extra-territorial association of persons; the absolute authority of the master of the "house," the father, gives way to the concept of public power ruling the life of a society. When urban life begins to proliferate into innumerable corporate cells, minds are naturally lifted to the conception of an order in which all the cells could be inter-connected, self-supporting and self-regulating. This order is most often conceived independently of any notion of territory.[46] The local churches themselves are regulated by their relations with the Apostolic See; it will thus be completely natural that religious groups likewise relate to their central authority.

At this time is established the theory of the State, holder of a public authority. Hereafter, the power is no longer the object of private property, and the right exercised by the prince is no longer patrimonial: his authority is public because it represents all the individuals who compose the society.[47] The object of his pursuit is

45. Cf. L. Moulin, "Les origines religieuses des techniques électorales et délibératives modernes," *op. cit.,* p. 107–117, and Carlo Guido Mor, *Le assemblee italiane del secolo X* (International Congress of Historical Sciences) 1950, University of Louvain, Collection of works, third series, fasc. 45, p. 24–25.

46. Cf. G. de Lagarde, *Individualisme et corporatisme au moyen âge,* L'organisation corporative du moyen âge à la fin de l'ancien régime, University of Louvain, Collection of works, second series, fasc. 44, 3–31.

47. Cf. G. de Lagarde, *Naissance de l'esprit laique au déclin du moyen âge,* t. I, 145–156. "At the end of the thirteenth century, two ideas are secured: to say that a power is public is to say that it realizes the general will, the common

none other than the general welfare or the common good. The legitimacy of a government is no longer judged according to conventional claims, but according to its conformity with the public welfare. Saint Thomas teaches that, in the midst of a unified group, the true sovereign is the common good; the sovereign is the social personality which incarnates the common good beyond all individual variations. The only sovereign is the social personality which guarantees the common good. Up until the thirteenth century,

> the most determined partisans of election reduced the latter to a simple designation of a nominee for an office which of itself, conferred the rights proper to the ruler. The genius of Saint Thomas is in having demonstrated the contrary, that no one could aspire to an inalienable right to power. No individual, race, collectivity, or even the whole multitude of citizens has any rights except those conferred by the harmony of its action with the common good.[48]

At the end of the thirteenth century, Henry of Ghent in his turn confirms that, instead of a patriarchal and domainal authority, the true principles of political science impose a collective authority, expressing the mind of the community which it rules. In this perspective, he who governs ceases to be a master or a father and tends to become a representative, or even a simple delegate of the community. If he goes counter to the common good, his subjects can legitimately resist, correct and depose him. From the eleventh and twelfth centuries, representative assemblies are seen rising up everywhere. The *praelatio* is the cornerstone of the Church, but the assertion is even made that there are limits to the power of prelates.[49]

---

pleasure of the people, and that it provides for the general welfare. . . . Authority ceases to be the result of a real or personal contract, linking the subject to a master in whom he had placed his faith: it appears as the instrument of a collective good." *ib.*, p. 157.

48. G. de Lagarde, *ib.*, III, 109.

49. Cf. G. de Lagarde, *La philosophie sociale d'Henri de Gand et de Godefroid de Fontaine*, L'organisation corporative du moyen âge à la fin de l'ancien régime, University of Louvain, Collection of works, third series, fasc. 18.

These ideas, which impregnated the whole world at that time, could not fail to penetrate as far as the cloister. It is not by chance that, well into the thirteenth century, the question was again raised concerning the abbot's authority which was precisely like that of the master of a house and a father: territorial and absolute. Thought is given to restricting the term of office to a limited number of years. This is the same mentality which renders the abbot responsible before the general chapter, a true, sovereign, social personality which guarantees the common good of the institute. And it is this very mentality which will yet end in replacing the lifetime abbot-prelates with changing superiors, elected for a few years only.

These ideas were all the more favorably received in the monastic world since their diffusion coincided with an evident weakening of the Christian spirit and an alarming invasion of secular values. The abbots, as has been seen, wasted religious goods and monopolized or distributed them among their relatives; or else they were negligent or incompetent in their administration. It is understood that the new social and political concepts served the legitimate discontent of religious in the face of these abuses. The resignations themselves did not offer satisfaction, since it was necessary to pay pensions to the retired abbots and meet the great expenses entailed by new provisions, as well as by the "services" exacted by the Roman Curia. Their multiplication, frequently at close intervals, was a convergent sign: if the abbots themselves retired so easily, was it not because the perpetual regime was no longer very firmly established? Was it not better to regulate the duration of the abbatial charge according to an average norm, rather than be exposed to the hazards of voluntary withdrawals or of depositions depending on a remote and disinterested authority? All these ideas and facts contributed to the disturbance of the ancient monastic organization and led to the temporary charge of the superior.

PART THREE

FROM THE FOURTEENTH TO THE
NINETEENTH CENTURY

CHAPTER EIGHT

THE DECADENCE OF THE MONASTERIES AND THE FIRST ATTEMPTS AT REFORM

THE THIRTEENTH CENTURY was already a century of decline: the fourteenth is one of decadence. Historians have sought to determine its origin and causes.[1] To those enumerated in the preceding chapter must be added still others, resulting from the greed of churchmen and the lessening of the religious spirit. The "expectancies" which gave a cleric the hope and the right to receive a benefice not as yet vacant, but which would become so at some indefinite future date, increased to such an extent that, from the pontificates of Urban IV and Clement IV, the ordinary collators were left to confer almost no benefices at all. Thus candidates for the abbatial office were multiplied without the least preoccupation with qualities required for such a function. To augment its resources, the Curia under Innocent IV constantly increased the "pontifical reserves"; destined at first for the benefices whose bearers had died in the Curia, they were enlarged and amplified, such that, from Clement V on, the Holy See interfered directly in abbatial nominations. The Curia profited by leaving the prelacies vacant as long as possible in order to handle the revenues; after having conferred the benefice, it received the "annates," consisting in a part of the revenues of the benefice which the collator gathered or retained during one or several years' time.

1. Cf. P. Schmitz, *Histoire de l'Ordre de saint Benoît, op. cit.,* III, 3-11, 42, 80; and G. Schnuerer, *L'Eglise et la civilisation au moyen âge, op. cit.,* III, 169-226.

Moreover, the Holy See often imposed as heads of abbeys religious from other orders or seculars.[2] The immediate consequence of this state of affairs was that the abbatial charge became the object of solicitations, intrigues and bargainings at the Roman court; there is not even a line drawn before violence, the accumulation of benefices, and simony.[3]

The usual worth of abbots thus appointed and the authority which they could have over their monks can easily be imagined.[4] Their authority was again lessened by the system of capitulations or promises to which the candidates were forced to agree before their election in order to forestall abuses or merely to restrain the initiatives of the chosen one. It will reach the point of completely forgetting the religious character of the abbot, spiritual father of his monks, in order to see only the external and advantageous side of the charge, springing from the more or less great wealth of the monastery or the importance of the "abbatial benefice." Never had the ecclesiastical and religious world as a whole been so profoundly ravished by a materialistic conception of life. Money and force were the two great powers which all obeyed. The secular world invaded every aspect of the religious society and ravished its spiritual life without hindrance. Under these conditions, what kind of guaranty could abbatial perpetuity still have? From the moment that the abbot is no more than an administrator of temporal goods and even, the greater part of the time, simply the beneficiary of a juridical title giving him the opportunity to indulge his own ambition and greed, there is no longer any need to assure his permanence until death. On the contrary, there can be a concern to see him changed as soon as possible, in the hope that his successor will be less proud and grasping. All the causes of monastic decadence prepare the way for temporary abbots.

2. Cf. U. Berlière, *Les élections abbatiales, op. cit.,* p. 23–28.

3. Cf. U. Berlière, *ib.,* 33–39.

4. It is under these same conditions that there was a multiplication of double elections, resulting from ambition and intrigue, fomented by the families or by the candidates themselves. These led to interminable and ruinous lawsuits.

The commendam is another consequence of this same spirit of greed. Originally, it consisted in the provisional protection and administration of a church or a monastery, on behalf of the benefice. But from the day when it was granted in the interests of the commendator, it became perpetual and was the source of great harm, given the fact that it attributed to a secular a regular benefice over which he had the same canonical rights and prerogatives as if he were a regular abbot. The new commendam dates from the thirteenth century and developed considerably during the course of the fourteenth, especially from the moment when, by virtue of the "apostolic reserves," the appointments to a great number of abbeys and priories were made directly by the Holy See.[5] The commendatory abbots were, for the most part, only interested in enjoying the revenues from the benefice; however, there were instances where they availed themselves of their spiritual rights to promote or facilitate the reforms. They were appointed for life, but they could resign.[6] The manner in which they behaved, added to the deep-seated flaws of the system, was one of the causes of the suppression of perpetual regular abbots, as will be seen. In fact, they were usually at the source of the material ruin and religious decadence of the monasteries.

To these various causes of decadence was added another. The religious spirit diminished within the monasteries in proportion to the increase of the number of sons of noble families who were driven there by their parents from their earliest youth, sometimes from infancy, and many of whom had no vocation. Such religious

5. "From the day when the Curia, short of funds, became accustomed to considering the monasteries as sources of revenues for its protégés, its familiars, and its courtisans, the commendam would assume an extraordinary extension and, due to the abuse which arose, would become a mortal wound in the monastic body—which was in some cases justified. Soon the Holy See even surrenders to sovereigns of such or such a country the charge of making appointments to vacant abbeys." P. Schmitz, *Histoire de l'Ordre de saint Benoit, op. cit.*, IV, 233; cf. R. Laprat, art. "Commende" in *Dictionnaire de Droit Canon*.

6. This was usually just a subterfuge to keep the commendam in the family, for they nearly always resigned in favor of a relative. Cf. P. Schmitz, *ib.*, IV, 237.

were incapable of making the necessary efforts to struggle against the decline and disgrace of which their houses were victim by reason of their leaders.

THE FIRST ATTEMPTS AT REFORM

Nevertheless, the healthy elements in the different orders and the responsible heads did not all remain inactive in face of these same disorders. From the twelfth century, the Benedictines imitated the Cistercians by instituting certain kinds of general chapters, uniting the abbots of a province.[7] The Lateran Council and Innocent III attempted to universalize this practice and impose it on all the monasteries. But this decision had little success, due to the lack of precision of many elements in the new institution, especially where coercive power was concerned; besides, the provincial chapters did not possess supreme power and left intact that of the bishops. The legislation which came out of these assemblies was improvised, hesitant, and had poor results. Honorius III confirmed and completed the work of his predecessor, chiefly by according a great importance to the canonical visitations, not hesitating to execute extraordinary ones by his legates or his apostolic visitators. Gregory IX again specified all of these measures and ordained that the provincial chapters should assemble every year, reinforcing the rules of enclosure, poverty, the common life, and insisting on the necessity of proper formation for the novices. He also recalled the abbot's duties: residence, common life, poverty, the obligation of explaining the Rule to his religious, and the duty of rendering accounts. The chapters continued to be held, and enacted numerous ordinances; but in spite of the severity of their decisions and sanctions, they remained a dead letter.

In the fourteenth century, Benedict XII, the austere Cistercian pope, tried again to check the evils. In 1336, he published the Bull,

---

7. The first were the abbots of the provinces of Reims, Saxony and Thuringia; they were imitated in Italy and in England, and finally throughout the rest of France and in Germany.

Summa Magistri Dignatio, a veritable plan of reform and unification. Unfortunately, for want of a hierarchical organization and a superior having sufficient authority to put it into practice, this document remained ineffective. The provincial chapters were impotent, and the visitators named by them could not be less so. The severe penal sanctions brought against transgressors did not suffice to save the Bull which remained almost without results. In addition, shortly afterwards, famine, the Black Plague, the Hundred Years' War and the peasant uprisings disorganized, depopulated and destroyed the monasteries, rendering all reform impossible.

Nevertheless, there were several realizations. In Spain, the monasteries of the province of Tarragona unite into a federation, to which are also joined those of the province of Saragossa. This union managed to preserve, in the thirteenth and at the beginning of the fourteenth century, a certain fervor in religious life, with regular chapters and visitations; but progress was halted by the commendam. At Cluny, the general chapters functioned regularly; but their authority was thwarted by that of the superior general, the abbot of Cluny, who retained his powers over dependent houses and over all the members of the Order.[8] The monasteries of Kastl and Melk were not organized into a congregation; there were no bonds between them other than a uniformity of rites and customs; there were neither general chapters nor periodical visitations. These movements too, animated by the best spirit and full of promise, had no effect. In England, the pontifical prescriptions on the reunion of general chapters and on the regular visitations were observed better than in any other country; the abbeys were nearly all dependent on the Ordinary, who jealously guarded the discipline and good administration.

All of these efforts were excellent, and the pontifical decisions

---

8. Nevertheless, the dependent abbots and priors had in fact become perpetual, as is testified in the Statutes of Henry I of Fautrières (1308–1319), promulgated at the general chapter of 1310. They could not be changed unless they had committed a grave fault, or else consented to retire. Cf. *Bibliot. Cluniac.,* 1562, C–D.

had the merit of attempting to make the general chapters elements of order and discipline, but they did not attack the root of the evil. The intervention in the abbatial appointments by factors alien to the monastic organization, the spirit of ambition and greed, the moral licence. All contributed at the same time to the ruin of the abbatial charge and the prevention of all true reform. It was necessary to make the communities independent with regard to the election of abbots, their recruiting, and their life, while still giving an effective authority to the general chapters. In the reform councils from the fourteenth to the sixteenth century, there is never any question of abbatial perpetuity; it is not this which creates the difficulty, but rather those who are invested with the abbatial charge. The reformed congregations will renounce the principle of perpetuity, not because it constituted an obstacle to reform, but because it entailed the interference of outside influences, all secular, at least in spirit. That is why, when the reform began in Italy, it was with the suppression of the commendam and of the commendatory abbots.

CHAPTER NINE

THE CONGREGATION OF SAINT JUSTINE OF PADUA AND ITS WORK OF REFORM

THE DECADENCE ATTAINED its maximum pitch during the period of the Council of Constance (1414–1418). And it was then that reform began.[1] Louis Barbo, already the commendatory abbot and reformer of the monastery of Saint Georges in Alga at Venice, received the Commendam of the abbey of Saint Justine of Padua. Taking his role seriously, he made profession in the Order of Saint Benedict, received the abbatial blessing in February 1409, and took possession of his abbey. To prevent it from again becoming a commendam, his first care was to ask the pope that, in the future, the abbots of Saint Justine be canonically elected by the religious and that they be confirmed *ipso facto* by the Holy See, without other formality: this latter was in order to avoid any intervention of the Curia. This privilege was successively confirmed by Martin V, Eugene IV, Sixtus IV, Alexander VI, Julius II and Leo X.[2] Another effective remedy against the commendam and outside intrusions into the govern-ment and administration of the new institution was grouping into

1. The Celestine and Olivetan Orders had already paved the way by a strict grouping of monasteries, but also by suppressing the abbatial charge in the dependent houses and reducing the abbot general's term to a fixed length of time. The Congregation of Cervara also had at the head of each of its houses merely a prior who was re-eligible only after an interval.

2. On the origins of the congregation, see T. Lecissotti, osb, *Miscellanea Cassinese*, vol 16, Introduction and p. 67, 70.

a congregation whose supreme authority was the general chapter;[3] it would name four visitors, one of whom would be "president."[4] The abbots were responsible before the general chapter, which could depose or merely suspend them if it deemed that they were *minus sufficientes vel idonei,* until they were acknowledged to be more efficient by the visitors. This was a trifle close to resuming the practice already existing in nearly all of the centralized orders. The chapter of 1425 established that the priors of dependent monasteries could only be confirmed for five years in the same monastery; after this time, they should surrender the charge, save for exceptional cases and with the consent of two-thirds of the definitors. Officially, nothing had changed for the abbots; but it appeared more and more clearly that they were merely delegates to the general chapter. According to Barbo, this is the reason why the three abbeys which had at first joined the reform later separated from it (1428–1429). Following this departure, the new congregation no longer accepted old monasteries except on condition that their superiors be annual. Eugene IV, by a Bull in 1432 and 1434, sanctioned the definitive statutes. The general chapter was proclaimed the supreme authority, from which emanated all other authority; it was annual, composed of superiors and delegates from the communities. During the chapter, all prelacies were suspended. It elected a definitory of nine members, of whom three were monks and six superiors. The committee of definitors had to provide for the selection of abbots, priors and visitors, with the option of changing them at will. From among the visitors who numbered five or six, this same committee chose one who performed the function of head of the congregation with the title of president. The abbots were annual, but could be renewed; in fact, according to the Acts of the general chapters, it is seen that they

3. Meanwhile, Louis Barbo had founded dependent priories, and three abbeys had been incorporated into Saint Justine.

4. This organization was sanctioned at the outset by a Bull from Martin V in 1419. The abbeys retained their abbots, elected by the community and perpetual, but the monks of the whole congregation were united among themselves in such a way that they formed only "one single family."

rarely remained several years consecutively at the head of the same monastery. They were easily transferred from one house to another; if they ceased to be superiors, they kept the title of abbots and their insignia. All the superiors fulfilled their functions merely in the capacity of representatives of the chapter and rendered to it an account of their charge.[5]

All these details are necessary if we wish to understand how the notion of annual abbots was reached. The immediate cause was a crisis which occurred after the Bull of Martin V, motivated by the susceptibility and the authoritative character of the first abbots. The remote causes were the unworthiness or incompetence of too many abbots, the interferences of the Curia and the princes in abbatial nominations, and lastly the commendam.[6] Gradually, the length of time between chapters and the duration of the abbatial charge were extended. The general chapters only assembled every two years from 1660, every three years from 1680, and every six years since 1852. The abbots remained in office from one chapter to the next. They were always temporary; they were not re-eligible, whereas the definitors and visitators were so indefinitely. Thus was recovered some of the stability, procured by perpetuity in the regime of the congregation; it was in the logic of a system where the autonomous subject is no longer the monastery, but the organism which groups all the houses to form one single body. The major superior is no longer the abbot of each house, but the regime, the committee of definitors or the general chapter, according to the letter of the constitutions. It is not very exact to say that the reform of Saint Justine originates from the action taken by Louis Barbo to avoid the abuses of evil or incompetent abbots, which prevented the power from being in the hands of one man

5. Eugene IV granted the new congregation the greatest freedom and most ample exemption, with all kinds of privileges. None of his monasteries, in the future, could be given in commendam.

6. Louis Barbo declares that he has departed from the principle of perpetual abbots because he saw no other means of wresting the monastic order from the fatal disaster of the commendam. *De initio et progressu congregationis Cassinensis*, c. VII, in Pez, *Thesaurus anecdot.*, II, p. III, p. 289.

I

alone, or the congregation from having as head one single monastery. It seems rather that it was to assure the whole of his reform
that he grouped all of his monasteries into one very stable central
organization, composed of a certain number of individuals elected
at rather brief intervals. If the dependent abbeys had abbots named
for one year, this was only a consequence.[7] Likewise, rather than
see Louis Barbo drawing his inspiration from the mendicant
orders, it is perhaps more exact to recognize that he merely drew
the conclusion of the concept of a religious order as applied to
Benedictine monasteries. Since Cluny had removable priors in its
dependent houses, the Carthusians priors responsible before the
general chapter, the Hermits of Saint Augustine triennial priors,
and since the needs of the Italian reform obliged the monasteries
to group themselves into a congregation, thus becoming similar
to religious orders, it was logical that the abbots of the various
monasteries of the congregation be elected by the central power
and at its discretion. And because the supreme authority resided
with the general chapter, the appointments which it made were
valid from one chapter to the next.

In addition, it must be noted that this solution was imperative
only in the countries where the commendam reigned and where
the causes of decadence occasioned by it were most violently
manifest: Italy, France, Spain, Portugal and England. The German
countries which had preserved themselves from this abuse waited
a long time before seeing the first congregation formed. The
federalist system prevailed with the autonomy of abbeys and
perpetual abbots elected by the communities.

7. The partisans of different reform movements all saw in the commendam
and in the multiplication of regular benefices the origin of laxity in the
monasteries. In order to stop it short, they drew inspiration from the organization of the mendicant orders in suppressing the perpetual abbots. The secular
prelates in the abbeys stood in support of perpetuity and consistorial nomination. The new congregation and those inspired by it replaced perpetuity with
the appointment of temporary superiors during the course of the general
chapter, whose power was a guaranty against internal weaknesses and external
abuse. Cf. P. Schmitz, *Histoire de l'Ordre de saint Benoit, op. cit.,* IV, 241.

THE REFORMED CONGREGATIONS OUTSIDE OF ITALY

In Spain, Vallodolid was founded at the same time that the reform of Louis Barbo was taking root (1390). In about 1436, its observance began to find its way into other abbeys; but the great period of extension only dates from the end of the fifteenth century, during the reign of Ferdinand and Isabella.[8] At the outset, it was a matter of a simple federation of monasteries adopting common usages. From the beginning, however, the abbatial charge was suppressed with a view toward avoiding the commendam, but the priors were perpetual. They became triennial in 1465, then were elected for six years, and finally, the duration of their term was reduced to four years. They were elected by the monks. In 1489, Innocent VIII declared the priors of the monastery of Vallodolid to be heads of the congregation, with the right to confirm the superiors of the other monasteries. Later on, these latter no longer wished to have a general who was not elected by them: at that time the generalate and the priorate of Vallodolid were separated.[9] In 1497, Alexander VI authorized the resumption of the abbatial title with all of its privileges. Eugene IV would have liked the new congregation to follow the constitutions of Saint Justine; he had to give up this idea, but in both cases the spirit was the same and the reform was similar. Here also, it was less a question of providing against abbatial perpetuity than against the commendam. According to the Constitutions of 1575, the abbots were elected every six years by the definitory; but at the time of the visitation, which takes place every three years, the visitators could begin proceedings for a new election.[10]

In Portugal, after an unsuccessful attempt at reform in the fifteenth century, a congregation instituted by Pius V in 1564 set itself up on the same pattern as Valladolid. The perpetuity of abbots

8. Cf. P. Schmitz, *ib.*, III, 234–235.

9. Cf. P. Schmitz, *ib.*, III, 236.

10. Cf. *Constituciones de los monces de la Congregacion de S. Benito de Valladolid,* Barcelona 1575, p. 65.

was abolished; these were appointed for three years and subject to the authority of the general whose own term was fixed at three years. Gregory XIII re-established the perpetual abbatial charge.[11]

The Council of Basle (1431–1439) marks the beginning of renewal in the Order of Saint Benedict, which was to end in the union of Bursfeld in Saxony, Thuringia, along the Rhine and the Moselle. It did not constitute a congregation like those in Italy and Spain, but a simple federation where each monastery kept its autonomy and its perpetual abbot; moreover, since most of the German monasteries were not exempt, they remained under the jurisdiction and control of the bishops. Nevertheless, this union did have general chapters: the first was convened in 1446. The abbot of Bursfeld was elected by the community and nine electors from other monasteries. He was the perpetual president of the union and the visitator general. He held jurisdiction over all the monks of the union and, between chapters, he had the powers necessary for resolving urgent questions with two assistant abbots and one assessor. The general chapter was annual, and it elected two definitors, two co-presidents, and the visitators. At the outset of each chapter, the abbots came forth to accuse themselves of their faults and, protesting their incompetence, asked to be relieved of their charge. Historians interpret this gesture in the sense of a purely ascetical practice. They add that these resignations were never accepted and that, if it was necessary to proceed against an abbot to have him deposed, recourse was had to the bishop, without making a point of the resignation.[12] In any case, it is certain that the

11. Cf. P. Schmitz, *Histoire de l'Ordre de saint Benoit, op. cit.*, III, 240 and IV, 169.

12. Cf. P. Schmitz, *ib.*, III, 192–193. The *Caeremoniale Bursfeldense* of 1474–1475 says: "Postremo singuli praelati et rectores de suis negligenciis publice coram tota congregacione illa de culpis et negligenciis suis se pro-clamare et absolutionem ab officio prelature et regiminis sue petere teneantur, ad regimem monachorum, quibus presunt, se insufficientes fore et idoneos humiliter contestantes." The first draft of the Statutes of 1250 gives a formula of the oath to be taken by the abbots of monasteries desiring to enter into the reform: the abbot promises to make this gesture at each chapter; the text follows: ". . . de absolutione abbacialis officii et dignitatis singulis annis

union of Bursfeld was not in favor of resignations which were multiplying in Germany as a result of the wars, difficulties of all kinds, and the reform. It is against this trend that a treatise was published: *De renuntiatione praelatorum*.[13]

We see the difference that existed between the congregations of Saint Justine and of Bursfeld on the subject of abbots. The former had radically suppressed perpetuity and had the superiors appointed by the definitory; the latter preserved elected and perpetual superiors, while still taking certain precautions, such as the possibility of eventual acceptance of a resignation by the general chapter. In fact, it was the conception of grouping into congregations with temporary abbots which was the most widespread, but with a tendency toward return to the election and perpetuity of abbots. After a century of fervor, the union of Bursfeld, federalist in nature, went into decline. Protestantism made a great number of houses disappear; but also the dissensions, to which the authority of the president and the general chapter could merely offer a very weak resistance, led to the separation of several monasteries and the creation of new groups. Besides, the princes and bishops did not favor the union of abbeys.[14]

In France, Cluny was in complete decline from the middle of the fourteenth century. In spite of an attempt at reform at the end of the century, the abbey was ruled by commendatory abbots from 1529.

---

petenda et ea juxta vota patrum predicti capituli concessa suis in locis acceptanda nec non de resistencia contra predicta non facienda sive procuranda per alios non utenda. . . ." Cf. P. Volk, *Die Generalkapitels-Rezesse der Bursfelder Kongregation,* Siegburg, 1955–1959, I, p. 29. The Statutes of 1700 say, in a still more explicit manner: "Juramenta abbatum, cum se congregationis obstringunt, et eorum resignationes de consilio capituli suscipit (Praeses), aut exigente ratione ab officio et judicio ejusdem capituli amovet." (*ib.,* p. 41); and a little farther on, in the same Statutes: "Si vero auditis aliorum P. P votis ab officio destituendus judicetur, ille vi voti congregationi facti, humiliter annuat, et in manus ordinis et Fratrum suorum de conventu resignet." (*ib.,* p. 48). This hardly resembles a simple formality.

13. Cf. P. Volk, *ib.,* II, 1531–1653; and *Revue d'Histoire Ecclésiastique,* 53 (1958), 586.

14. Cf. P. Schmitz, *Histoire de l'Ordre de saint Benoit, op. cit.,* IV, 133–141.

The general chapters ceased to assemble in 1571. There was thus no change in the mode of government, nor in the lifetime character of the abbatial charge.[15]

The Pragmatic Sanction (1438) had indeed re-established electoral freedom in conventual abbeys and priories, abolished the annates, the reserves and the "expectancies"; but it stipulated that the king could "recommend" a candidate to the electors. It was a relapse into the evil ways of old. The Concordat of 1516 concluded at Bologna only served to place the pope and the king in agreement concerning the interventions of the prince, and thus more surely annul the freedom of the electors.[16] Meanwhile, however, in 1479, the abbey of Chezal-Benoît undertook a reform. Among other decisions, the abbot, Peter of Mas, himself renounced the perpetuity of the abbatial charge and subjected himself to a new election every three years. In 1488, he laid down and published statutes inspired by those of Saint Justine.[17] The congregation which bore the name of the monastery of Chezal-Benoît was formed between 1499 and 1502; the first general chapter was held in 1505–1506. It promulgated the statutes and appointed the abbots. This was a kind of compromise between the system of Bursfeld and that of Saint Justine; from the former, Chezal-Benoît kept the principle of federation, from the latter, it took the notion of temporary abbots appointed by the general chapter. The Concordat of 1516 interrupted its activity by attributing the appointment of abbots to the king.

The Congregation of Exempts, also known as Gallican, founded in 1579, anticipated in its statutes that the superior general could suspend the local superiors and even deprive them of their charge; but nearly all the abbots were commendators.[18]

In Spain, the Congregation of Claustrales continued to live according to the constitutions of 1361 until Clement VIII reformed

15. Cf. P. Schmitz, *ib.*, III, 145–150; 207–208; IV, 53.
16. Cf. P. Schmitz, *ib.*, III, 202–204.
17. Cf. P. Schmitz, *ib.*, III, 209.
18. Cf. P. Schmitz, *ib.*, IV, 12–13.

them by a Bull in 1592. But this latter was only accepted in 1661, and the constitutions of 1662 are the first that take the reform into account. They anticipated a general chapter every three years, with presidents, definitors and visitators elected for the same length of time. There were three presidents, four visitators, and the definitory was composed of four abbots and eight monks; the abbots were elected by the community and perpetual.[19] In 1602, Clement VIII approved the "Benedictine Mission" in England, that is the sending of English monks, who had been trained in the Congregations of Saint Justine and Valladolid, into this country as missionaries, and he associated the Mission with Valladolid. Monasteries were founded in various countries to serve as seminaries for the Mission. In 1609, they attached themselves to the old English congregation which consisted of only one monk. In 1633, the Mission separated from Valladolid to form a new congregation. All power belonged to the general chapter which assembled every four years; it appointed the superiors when those who were in office submitted their resignations. In the case of a vacancy between two chapters, the prior was elected by the community. The president did not govern any community.[20]

In Germany and Switzerland, despite various attempts at reform and grouping into congregations, the situation remained unchanged.[21] Each group had its own proper observances, but most of them followed the constitutions of Bursfeld on fundamental points, especially with regard to the election of perpetual abbots

19. Cf. P. Schmitz, *ib.*, IV, 166–167. Chapter VI of title IX, indicating the order of precedence at the general chapter, has this beginning: "Per gradus dignitatum discretus proportionabiliter personarum ordo, ad exemplar triumphantis Hyerusalem, pulsa confusione, rutilat. . . ."

20. Cf. P. Schmitz, *ib.*, IV, 113–115. The superiors bear the titles of *praeses, provincialis, definitor, prior, praepositus;* there is no question of abbots, but the provincials and priors are likened to them. The cathedral priors are perpetual, but they must, *"pro more Bursfeldensis congregationis,"* offer their resignation at each chapter, which can accept it *"si causa justa capituli generalis judicio appareat."* Cf. *Constitutiones Missionis Benedictinorum Congregationis Anglicanae,* Douai, 1633, p. 60.

21. Cf. P. Schmitz, *ib.*, IV, 117–147.

by the community.[22] In Austria, the abbots were likewise elected for life.[23]

The Camaldolese, in the constitutions of 1649, which rather closely reproduce those of 1520 drawn up by Blessed Giustiniani, established that the general chapter would be convened every year, or at least every three years, according to the customs of the different congregations. Here will be elected the definitory, *supremus magistratus,* which will have supreme authority and which will appoint the superiors after having released those who are currently in office.[24]

In the Order of Vallombrosa, from the end of the fifteenth century, after having abandoned perpetual abbots, a system of definitors is adopted, elected by the general chapter, with full authority to legislate, judge, and name superiors. After 1540, the Order has at its head a president elected for three years, who cannot be the abbot of Vallombrosa. Since 1572, he receives the title of general and is a titular abbot. In 1574, the duration of the generalate was extended to four years. At the present time, the abbot general is in office for twelve years and he has reclaimed the title of abbot of Vallombrosa.[25]

In the Order of Cîteaux, there is general fidelity to the ancient structure. But there is careful consideration of the abbots; their fidelity to their obligations is watched and there is no reluctance in proceeding to the deposition of incompetent or unworthy in-

22. In the Congregation of Bavaria, besides the definitory or directory composed of a president, two visitators and an assistant abbot, the president named three auditors to examine the accounts of the monasteries. Moreover, the abbots and the delegates of houses (one for each monastery) assembled separately; the two meetings communicated between themselves through the agency of the chapter secretary.

23. Cf. *Regula S. Patris Benedicti, una cum constitutionibus Congregationis Austriacae Monasteriorum Ordinis ejusdem S. Benedicti,* 1626. The general chapter took place every two years and, each time, elected the president, the chancellor and one visitator per province.

24. *In Regulam divi Patris Benedicti declarationes et constitutiones Patrum Ordinis Camaldulensium,* Venice, 1649, p. 246 and 259.

25. Cf. F. Tarani, *L'ordine Vallombrosano, Note storicochronologiche,* Florence, 1921.

dividuals.[26] This is done by the Father-abbot or by his vicar, with the assistance of three other abbots. As for resignations, from 1438 on, they can be made directly into the hands of the pope in a secret consistory, without need of the general chapter's consent. A few years later in 1442, the general chapter declares that this privilege is not detrimental to the rights of the Father-abbots. Finally, Innocent VIII (1482–1492) modifies the privilege by deciding that the resignation into the hands of the pope cannot take place except with the agreement of the abbot of Cîteaux or the general chapter.[27] From the moment when there was a vicar general of the Order, in the seventeenth century, the Father-abbot seems to have required his consent in order to accept a resignation.[28] The usual authority for receiving the resignation, then, has always been the Father-abbot; the general chapter only intervened to give its approval after the Father-abbot had received the resignation, or else it gave him permission to receive it. As for changes of abbey, Martin V established, in 1417, that no abbot could abandon the government of his monastery to take on another without the permission of the general chapter and the consent of the Holy See.[29] Thus, on the whole, the Cistercians remained firmly attached to the principle of a lifetime abbatial charge, while still keeping a strict control on the government of the abbots.

Nevertheless, there were exceptions. In Spain, the Congregation of Castile, product of the reformer Martin of Vargas, suppressed the abbots and replaced them with triennial priors. But the difficulties which resulted, especially the processes occasioned by the frequency of elections, led to a return to perpetual abbots.[30] In

26. See, for example, the text of the general chapter of 1601, XXI, 16; Canivez, VII, 226.

27. Cf. Noschitzka, *Die kirchenrechtliche Stellung des resignierten Regularabtes*, *op. cit.*, p. 65; Canivez, 1442, 72. Examples of resignation into the hands of the pope, with the consent of the general chapter, in Canivez, 1501, 14 and 1521, 24.

28. Cf. Noschitzka, *ib.*, p. 67.

29. Cf. Noschitzka, *ib.*, p. 54.

30. Cf. Canivez, art. "Cîteaux," *Dictionnaire de Droit Canon*; and *Statuta capitularium generalium*, 1516, 66; 1517, 17; 1524, 21.

Italy, the Congregation of Lombardy and Tuscany, founded in
1597, in Portugal, the Congregation of Alcobaça, founded in 1567,
and in France, the Congregation of Feuillants, instituted in 1586:
all had triennial abbots. The Congregation of Aragon, founded in
1616, had abbots for four years. The Roman Congregation, in 1623,
had temporary abbots, perhaps annual at the outset and then
triennial. There was also a Congregation of Calabria and Lucania,
founded in 1605, which suppressed the existence of monasteries
sui iuris and perpetual abbots. All of these congregations disappeared
at the time of the French Revolution or at the beginning of the
nineteenth century.

A sincere desire for reform, as well as the example of success
given by Saint Justine and its union, encouraged monasteries almost
everywhere, especially in the Latin countries and in England, to
find the principle of their renewal in a monastic regrouping, no
longer on the very broad scale of medieval Christianity, but on the
more restricted scale of nationalities. On the one hand, this re-
organization was at least remotely inspired by the centralization of
absolute monarchies; on the other, the separatist tendencies were
emphasized in the organization of the various nations. The fact
that the new centralized orders were formed in national provinces
was not without influence on the formation of different monastic
congregations from the end of the fifteenth to the eighteenth
century. It is as a consequence of the foundation of these congregations
that, in Italy, Spain, Portugal, France and England, the perpetual
abbatial charge often came to be suppressed, whereas the German-
speaking countries, on the whole, preserved it.

It is not without interest to note that, during the same period and
in the same countries where the perpetual abbatial charge is being
suppressed, the Society founded by Saint Ignatius of Loyola (d.
1556) opts for the lifetime superiorate in the person of the general.
The constitutions of the Society specify that this decision was
made after mature deliberation, and give the reasons which
motivated it: the lifetime superiorate allows the bearer to acquire
a great experience of affairs and of men, which can only be given
by a prolonged exercise of power; examples of perpetuity are

offered by the pope, the bishops and the princes; frequent elections include the risk of seeing occasions of intrigue and personal ambition arise, *quae huius modi officiorum pestis est;* finally, it is easier to find a man fit to exercise the power at long intervals than to locate one every three or four years. The general will thus enjoy a more stable authority if he is not removable than if he changes at the end of a few years.[31]

31. Cf. *Monumenta Ignatiana ex autographis vel ex antiquioribus exemplis collecta,* third series, *S. Ignatii de Loyola constitutiones Societatis Jesus,* t. III, p. 242–243.

CHAPTER TEN

THE FRENCH CONGREGATIONS OF THE
SEVENTEENTH CENTURY

O F THE NUMEROUS CONGREGATIONS
formed after that of Saint Justine, the two most important
ones remain to be considered. In general, congregations
founded since the sixteenth century drew inspiration for their statutes
from the admonitions given by the Council of Trent; but mainly,
they had issued from the same movement of reform and were
penetrated by the same spirit as the foundation of Louis Barbo.
Also, they often took as a base the constitutions and customs of
Saint Justine. Some were parallel movements which had nothing
in common among themselves but the broadest principles; others
had been born one from the other, and were like reforms of
reforms. Such is the case of Saint Vanne and Saint Maur.

The Society of Brittany, detached in 1603 from the abbey of
Marmoutier of the Congregation of Exempts, will in turn unite
with Saint Maur and be absorbed by it. It had been composed of
the abbey of Saint Denis and several monasteries of Exempts. Each
year on the Monday of Passion Week, the superiors, who no
longer had the title of abbots, resigned their charge in the presence
of the community; the day after Palm Sunday, a new election was
held. The superiors were re-eligible.[1]

At Saint Vanne, the reform began in 1598; the new congregation
was instituted in 1608. The Bull of Clement VIII declared it to be

---

1. Cf. P. Schmitz, *Histoire de l'Ordre de Saint Benoit, op. cit.,* IV, 13–16.

ad instar congregationis Cassinensis.[2] It thus took as a model the Constitutions of Saint Justine, often reproducing them verbatim. In the new foundation, the sovereign authority resided with the general chapter which was held every year and proceeded to the election of the president and the nomination of superiors. The former only remained in office one year, the latter five years. Since most of the abbeys were in commendam, the superiors merely had the title of priors; nevertheless, they were comparable to the abbots of the Cassinese Congregation. There still existed a few regular abbeys whose abbots were monks. This is how there came to be an abbot at Saint Leopold of Nancy: he was elected for five years as there was no perpetual superior. From 1744, the general chapter no longer took place every three years, the length of time which parallels the duration of the superior's charge. The priors of monasteries could have their charge renewed, but only once.[3] There seems to have been a preoccupation with the dangers resulting from the superior's long term in office; this led, at the time, beyond the idea of a temporary superior, renewable as often and as long as he was useful to the order, to that of a superior whose charge was strictly limited to a very brief period.

After having spread throughout France, this reform penetrated into Belgium and gave rise to the Congregation of the Presentation of Our Lady, founded in 1628 with constitutions modeled on those of Saint Vanne. The general chapter was annual, with the election of a president for five years and visitators for three years. Visitations were annual. A major difference in relation to Saint Vanne is that the new congregation kept abbots and they remained perpetual. It must not be forgotten that, in Belgium, a great number of abbeys formed part of the union of Bursfeld which had also preserved the lifetime abbatial regime. All these monasteries like-

2. Dom Didier de la Cour and Dom Claude Francis his auxiliary had gone to Italy and been impressed by the regular observance of the Cassinese monasteries of Saint Justine. Moreover, Rome sent to the cardinal of Lorraine, promoter of the reform, a counselor in the person of Dom Lawrence Lucalberti, a monk of the Cassinian Congregation.

3. Cf. P. Schmitz, *Histoire de l'Ordre de saint Benoit, op. cit.,* IV, 22–25.

wise remained under the jurisdiction of the Ordinary. From this fact there arose difficulties which led to the suspension of the chapters and the end of the Congregation.[4]

The Congregation of Saint Vanne having reformed several monasteries in France, these latter finished by uniting to form a separate institution which assumed the name of Saint Maur. Founded in 1618, it was canonically established by a Bull from Gregory XV in 1621: *"ad instar Cassinensis erecta et regenda."* At the outset, it simply and solely preserved the Constitutions of Saint Vanne. The general chapter of 1621 even examined a decree of the latter, proposing the union of the two congregations under the same general residing in Rome, with assistants or assessors of provinces, and provincials; this general would have been elected for five years, the assistants for three years, and the provincials for two years. This organization reflected that of the Jesuits, the Discalced Carmelites and the Feuillants.[5] The decree was rejected by the chapter that was held at Jumièges.

At the general chapter of 1622 held at Corbie, the president was re-elected, remaining annual until 1628, and the Congregation was divided into two provinces.[6] In 1623, the "regulations drawn up on the advice of Cardinal de la Rochefoucault for the union of the Order of Cluny and the Congregation of Saint Maur" stated that the general of the union would exercise his function for five years, but that he could be re-elected "as long as it would be deemed expedient by the general chapter"; besides, he could be deposed by an extraordinary chapter. The project was not pursued.[7]

4. Cf. P. Schmitz, *ib.,* IV, 97–98.

5. ". . . and to accomplish this (the union of the two congregations), it will be fitting to gather information on the forms and customs observed among the Jesuit Fathers, the Discalced Carmelites and the Feuillants, for the creation and election of similar superiors and officers." E. Martène, *Histoire de la Congrégation de Saint-Maur,* ed. Dom Charvin, Ligugé, 1928–1943, I, p. 101 and n. 2. This testimony is important for explaining the evolution of the question of superiors in the two congregations. Rather than the given facts of monastic tradition, recourse is had to the practice of modern orders and congregations. It is not surprising that it ended in the suppression of the perpetuity of abbots themselves.

6. Cf. E. Martène, *ib.,* I, 121.   7. Cf. E. Martène, *ib.,* I, 144.

The general chapter of 1623 held at Saint Faron proceeded to the confirmation of the outgoing president, and appointed Dom Maur du Pont visitator in the province of Aquitaine and the prior of Saint Augustine of Limoges abbot of the monastery after the resignation of Dom Jean Regnaud. Appointed by the general chapter and according to the king's favor, these abbots were temporary, subject to the will of the general chapter.[8]

The chapter of 1630 held at Vendome approved the new constitutions, which were merely an adaptation of those of Saint Vanne and, consequently, also those of Saint Justine. The general chapters would now be only triennial, whereas the visitations would remain annual. The president received the title of general, and he was elected for three years, just as the superiors of the monasteries. The former could be re-elected indefinitely; the latter, on the contrary, were only re-eligible once and, after a maximum of six years in office, had to be replaced. However, they could be named prior in another monastery.[9] At the following chapter, held at Vendome in 1633, the number of definitors was raised to nine.[10]

Thus the constitutions continued to be revised and adjusted according to the lessons of experience. It was only at the chapter of Vendome in 1645 that they received definitive approbation, after which they were published.[11] The general chapter was declared to have the legislative and executive power; its authority was sovereign and it handled appointments to all the offices of the Congregation. It would convene every three years and elect nine definitors who had a deliberative voice concerning the whole congregation and who named all the superiors, including the general and the officers of the Congregation. The influence of Saint Justine is recognized here. The superior general, elected for three years and re-eligible in perpetuity, remained subject to the general chapter. Besides

8. Cf. E. Martène, *ib.*, I, 148–149 and 201.
9. Cf. E. Martène, *ib.*, II, 2.
10. Cf. E. Martène, *ib.*, II, 41, n. 4.
11. Cf. E. Martène, *ib.*, III, 18–19.

himself, the regime was composed of two assistants and six visitators, one per province. These latter, like the priors of the monasteries, could not remain in charge more than six years in the same office. Each year, there was a reunion of the diet, composed of members of the regime. The general chapter included the members of the regime and four superiors named by the diet of each province. Several abbeys, coming from the Congregation of Chezal-Benoît, retained the abbatial title, but the bearer was appointed by the general chapter and for the same term of office as the priors.[12]

The text of the constitutions still maintained the name of abbot and that of prelate, but this was nothing more than a vestige, the words serving merely to designate the regular superiors who had an ordinary jurisdiction. No longer do any of these bear the insignia nor enjoy the *pontificalia;* not one of them was perpetual. But most important, their authority was strictly limited on behalf of the visitators, the provincials, the superior general, the definitory and the general chapter. Saint Maur then went further than Saint Justine by suppressing the abbots and replacing them with superiors appointed for a very brief term. However, the Congregation returned, after an experience of ten years, to a more traditional conception, admitting that the superior general could be confirmed and his functions prolonged without time limit if the interests of the Congregation required it. Dom Tarisse remained thus in office until his death. The importance of the new disposition was well perceived at the time; it also aroused a certain opposition, under the pretext that it was straying from the customs of Saint Justine which, according to the Bull of institution, should serve as model and rule.[13] In reality, this return to a certain stability and continuity in the government of the superior general was one of the causes of the success and fecundity of the new Congregation.

12. Cf. P. Schmitz, *Histoire de l'Ordre de saint Benoit, op. cit.,* IV, 33–38.

13. This refers to the opposition and intrigues of Dom Faro of Chalus, abbot of Seez, and his supporters. Cf. F. Rousseau, *Dom Grégoire Tarisse* (Pax Collection, XV), Paris, 1924, p. 64–69.

THE TEACHING OF THE CANONISTS

It is interesting to look at the thinking of the canonists at the moment when the Congregation of Saint Maur sanctioned the result of the reform movement begun by Louis Barbo, and ended with the suppression of the perpetuity of the abbatial charge itself. Martino de Azpilcueta, called Navarrus (1492–1586), criticizes the triennial elections and concludes in this manner:

> Et consequenter non solum videtur non extendenda haec triennalis mutatio, sed valde vitanda, ut caritas, et humilitas, unitas et mansuetudo servetur.[14]

Suarez, for his part (1548–1617), writes:

> When the prelacy is conferred by electoral vote, it is morally advisable that it be either perpetual or for a very long term, because of the inconveniences and dangers of elections. These evils seem so intrinsic, considering human frailty and experience, that they appear more difficult to avoid than those which ordinarily accompany perpetuity.[15]

The question of perpetual abbots is treated *ex professo* by Tamburini (d. 1666). First of all, he concedes that the abbots are not perpetual by divine right, nor by a positive common law, but that they are by virtue of a negative common law in the sense that the common law is in no way opposed to it.[16] On the contrary, he adds that each time that there is mention of the abbatial charge, no limit is assigned to it. Moreover, the abbots are elected and by common law, all elective officers are perpetual. Finally, abbots cannot be deposed except for motives anticipated by the law, a

14. *Consiliorum sive responsorum libri quinque*, 1. III, de regular., Consil. LXXXII, n. 8; cf. *Dictionnaire de Droit Canon*, I, 54.

15. *Tractatus 8, De Religione*, 1. 2, c. 7, n. 8.

16. Cf. Tamburini, *De jure Abbatum et aliorum praelatorum*, t. I, disp. XII, p. 105.

K

condition which, according to common law, justifies perpetuity. Having posed these principles, Tamburini goes on to admit that, according to the particular law and de facto in a good number of the monastic congregations of his time, the abbots are temporary according to standards and customs fixed by constitutions.[17] In spite of the limits imposed on the duration of the charge, he considers that the abbatial dignity remains for life: he sees the proof of this in the practice of a certain number of congregations, who renew the abbots in their charge indefinitely or else transfer them as superiors to other monasteries. In a third question, Tamburini enumerates the reasons which militate in favor of perpetuity and those which are opposed to it. If the abbots were elected by their chapter for a determined length of time, they would be dependent, to a certain extent, on their subjects, and their authority would thus be lessened. Frequent changes stir up ambition; then come briberies, deceits, misunderstandings, factions and collusions, which are in opposition to fraternal charity and destroy the peace. In the Church, the usual practice is that bishops and prelates are perpetual. The positive reasons in support of perpetuity are not lacking: one who is charged with something for life becomes more attached and better devoted to it; a long experience favors good government.

Tamburini also enumerates the contrary reasons. The first is the practice which has arisen during his time. He considers that, if the ancient custom of the perpetual abbatial charge has been changed in such a universal manner, it is because experience has demonstrated its serious drawbacks. The popes were inclined to think so, since they supported this practice by approving the abandonment of the perpetual regime in favor of a temporal one, and never the reverse. These are the two main arguments. After what we have seen, they will not appear very convincing. If there were hardly any perpetual abbots left in Italy, Spain and France in the seventeenth century, it was far from the same case in the Germanic

17. Tamburini is not very fortunate in the example he cites, that of the Cistercians. If, as has been seen, a certain number of Italian and Spanish congregations actually had temporary abbots, it was not the same in France.

countries. As for saying that the abbots are perpetual by virtue of a "negative common law," this is using an unfortunate expression which is also insufficient to characterize a situation so strongly supported by pontifical and conciliar texts and so explicitly recognized by ancient Canon Law.

Romelius (d. 1656) speaks out against the frequency of abbatial elections:

> Electiones triennales et temporales sunt seminarium, ex quo pullulant mille incommoda, ambitiones, conventiones simoniacae, subornationes et collusiones perpetuae, factiones et dissidia irrevocabilia, sussurationes, murmurationes, detractiones continuae, pax et concordia mala, sublatio vel certe enervatio disciplinae regularis et auctoritatis corrigendi praecipiendique, occasio ejiciendi vel relegandi suos adversarios in alia monasteria. . . .[18]

His contemporary Faganus (d. 1678) insists on the principle of the perpetuity of abbots who receive their monasteries rightfully and are the spouses of their church and of their monastery, in imitation of the bishops. This is why the decrees say that, at the death of the abbot, his church is a widow. He also adds that, according to the ancient law, by virtue of this bond which unites him with his monastery, the abbot, once blessed, cannot be transferred elsewhere without a dispensation from the pope.[19]

These few examples show that, at the moment when the reformed monastic congregations were being developed and propagated,[20] with temporary abbots, there were some canonists who continued to support the lifetime principle. The question was then far from

---

18. *Capita canonica de jure abbatum,* 1728, c. I, n. 10, cf. *Dictionnaire de Droit Canon* I, 54.

19. Cf. Faganus, *Comment. in Lib. Decretalium,* 1. I, tit, VI, c. 41.

20. Saint Peter Fourier reformed the Canons Regular of Lorraine and organized for them the Congregation of Notre-Sauveur; he became the superior general in 1632. He wanted this to be a lifetime charge. In the face of opposition from the Roman Curia, he finally declared that the general should be elected for at least twenty years. Cf. Fourier Bonnard, *Lettres choisies de saint Pierre Fourier,* Paris, 1918, p. 111 and 117.

being settled: in any case, it was not resolved. In actual fact, there continued to be perpetual abbots and, in the law, their position retained all of its force.

The eighteenth century brought with it, as an effect of well known causes, a weakening of the religious spirit and a decadence within institutions, followed by secularization, plundering, and then the suppression of houses with the dispersion of the religious. The abbots, even those who were not commendators, usually lived apart from the community and maintained the life style of noblemen. In fact, this, even more than the decadence, was the ruin and death of the monastic order. Dom Philibert Schmitz writes:

At the beginning of the nineteenth century, of the hundreds and thousands of Benedictine monasteries which had covered Christian Europe, there only remained about thirty.[21]

The situation was identical in the other monastic orders.

---

21. Cf. P. Schmitz, *Histoire de l'Ordre de saint Benoit, op. cit.,* IV, 175.

CHAPTER ELEVEN

THE MONASTIC RESTORATION OF THE
NINETEENTH CENTURY

IT IS NOT HERE a question of expounding the various attempts at restoration made by the ancient monastic orders or congregations, nor of writing the history of all the foundations made after the revolutionary tempest, with a view toward renewing the best of each order according to its tradition. We will not even strive for a complete enumeration of the monastic congregations. Only the customs of a certain number of them in regard to the regime of superiors will be noted. Since it is a matter of contemporary facts, it should not be difficult to complete the investigation.

The role played by Dom Gueranger in the restoration of the Order of Saint Benedict is well known. From the beginning, he would have wished to resume the lifetime regime of abbots. He could not obtain this from the Holy See all at once. On the one hand, the Roman Curia was still too much under the influence of all that transpired, especially in Italy, in recent centuries; on the other hand, the supreme authority wished to act prudently in the presence of an experiment which was still so new and very fragile. Perpetuity was granted only after three successive three year terms; the abbot of Solesmes thus became perpetual after a nine year temporary regime. According to the Constitutions of 1837, the abbots of monasteries who would come to join the new congregation would require four three year terms before they could become perpetual. The congregation lived under this regime until after the death of Dom Gueranger (1875). His successor Dom

Couturier was declared a perpetual abbot by the Brief of February 16, 1877 and dispensed from the three year terms. From 1879 on, these three year terms were suppressed for all the abbots of the congregation, who became perpetual as of their first election.[1]

In the Cassinese Congregation, formerly that of Saint Justine, which had survived the tempest, the general chapter, which was at first annual, had become triennial; in 1853, it was decided that, henceforth, it would meet every six years. It was always the chapter that appointed and transferred abbots, now every six years. In 1855, the government of Piedmont, under the new monarchy of Victor Emmanuel II, suppressed the religious congregations which were not engaged in hospital work or teaching. These measures were extended throughout the entire peninsula as the troops of the Risorgimento conquered Italian soil. At the general chapter of 1858, to avoid having recourse to the State with a view toward obtaining the *placet* for the nomination of new abbots, it was decided to ask the Holy See for the prolongation of the abbatial charge in the congregation. The abbots thus remained in office by virtue of an Apostolic Indult until 1915. At that time, the constitutions were changed and perpetuity was introduced.

Father Casaretto had been elected abbot of Saint Julian of Genoa in 1844 by the superiors of the Cassinese Congregation. In 1850 he was named abbot of Saint Scholastica of Subiaco by Pius IX; but this abbey preserved commendatory abbots. The following year, after the establishment of a dependent but distinct province composed of three monasteries, Dom Casaretto became the Visitator-abbot. New constitutions came into force in 1862. They provided for an abbot general, an abbot procurator general, and visitor abbots, each governing his own province; they were all elected for twelve years by the general chapter. The superiors of houses were elected by the provincial chapter with the title of priors for the important monasteries. If, in an exceptional case, it was desirable to

---

1. Cf. *Regula SS. Patris nostri Benedicti una cum constitutionibus congregationis S. Petri de Solesmis,* 1901, p. 180, 192; Rescript of July 26, 1879, Congr. of Bishops and Regulars, n. 17326. Cf. *Dictionnaire de Droit Canon,* I, 54–55, art. "Abbés."

place an abbot at the head of a monastery, he was elected by the general chapter for three years and was re-eligible. In 1867, the province was set up as an autonomous organism *ad experimentum* for ten years, which were later changed to five years; in 1872, it became the Cassinese Congregation of the Primitive Observance. At the chapter of 1880, it was decided that the abbots would be elected for life by their communities.[2] The abbey of Saint Scholastica at Subiaco had a commendatory abbot until the time of Leo XIII. It was effectively governed by the abbot general of the congregation. It was only under Pius X, that a Rescript finally approved the separation of the charge of abbot general from that of abbot of Saint Scholastica. A regular abbot of the monastery was elected that same year.

The English Benedictine Congregation has perpetual abbots by law; but, by virtue of a dispensation granted by Leo XIII on the request of interested parties, they are actually only elected for six, eight, ten or twelve years.[3]

In the Congregation of Beuron, the abbots have been perpetual since it began in 1868.

In America, the first Benedictine monastery, founded by Dom Boniface Wimmer at Saint Vincent in Pennsylvania, was established as an abbey with a perpetual abbot in 1855.[4]

Today, all Benedictine abbots are elected for life by their communities.[5]

Among the Cistercians of the Common Observance, most of the congregations of the sixteenth and seventeenth centuries had temporary abbots but they ceased to exist at the end of the eighteenth century or the beginning of the nineteenth. At present, out

2. "Abbates autem, sic electi et confirmati, monasterii regimen ad vitam retineant, praeterquam si ad majus aliquod munus nempe abbatis generalis vel procuratoris generalis assumantur ad praescriptum Constitutionum." *Constitutiones Patrum Congregationis Cassinensis a primaeva observantia,* c. V, n. 7, p. 182.

3. Cf. C. Butler, *Benedictine Monachism* (New York, Barnes and Noble, 1962), p. 238.

4. Cf. C. J. Barry, *Worship and Work,* Saint John's Abbey, 1956, p. 14.

5. Cf. Introduction, footnote (Tr.).

of ten congregations which compose the Order, two have abbots elected for six years: Saint Bernard in Italy and Senaque. The Congregation of Casamari has abbots elected for fifteen years, eighteen for the president. All the others have perpetual abbots. The Cistercians of the Strict Observance have never known other than perpetual abbots.

The Olivetans and the Premonstratensians have perpetual abbots, whereas the abbot general is elected for twelve years.

Thus the contemporary monastic restoration which has had the success and splendid development known for more than a century has, on the whole, favored a return to the principle of the abbot's election by his community and his perpetuity, either by maintaining these wherever they still existed or by re-establishing them as soon as possible.

THE DOCTRINE

These facts can find a basis in the doctrine set forth in the works of contemporary monastic authors. It will suffice to quote several texts from among the better known.

Dom Maur Wolter, the restorer of Beuron and the founder of the Congregation of the same name, writes in his *Praecipua Ordinis monastici elementa*:

If the abbot is truly the father of his monks, he completely satisfies all his duties. It also follows from this principle that the abbot is established for life and enjoys a perpetual authority and jurisdiction. This is indeed like natural fatherhood : it is not limited in time. The kinship that it creates is necessarily eternal, and the relation of father and son cannot be altered. This universal law seems to take on a special significance when it is a question of spiritual fatherhood, because the latter does not rest in the body but in the soul itself, and is associated with its immortality. That is why it is fitting to elect for life not only the fathers of the faithful (the pope, then the bishops and pastors), but also the fathers of the monks, in order that the monastic family may never be deprived of its own proper foundation.

. . . . It is just as important for the father to be stable as for the son . . . ; if this stability is lacking in one of them, in the father or the son, it becomes impossible for the family of God to remain safe from all harm. . . . From this fact springs the reciprocal devotion, paternal and filial, which so helps to attain the perfection of charity, a devotion which continues to grow from day to day to the maturity of a holy and unshakable love. . . . Lastly and above all, this immutability of the father, on the one hand, stifles the fatal ambition of men and does away with most of the obstacles which stand in the way of harmony and tranquillity ; on the other hand, it gives the abbot the motivation necessary for the pastor to undertake good works which demand much time and attention.[6]

It is interesting to note that this conception of spiritual fatherhood recalls the historical sources of the abbatial charge in the East.

Dom Besse declares that:

when the founders of the Congregations of Saint Justine, Valladolid and Saint Maur recognized the impossibility of reacting effectively against the abuses of the commendam, they sacrificed the principle of perpetuity. This violation of the letter and the spirit of the Rule . . . was explained by the circumstances which thwarted the Benedictine Order. . . . The motives which had imposed it have long since disappeared, and the monasteries are gradually returning to their time-honored tradition.[7]

Dom Delatte does not explicitly speak of our problem; but his thought appears clearly in his *Life of Dom Gueranger*, with regard to the approbation of the Constitutions of 1837:

Certain additional resolutions, intended to compromise with the spirit of the day, also removed from the principle of perpetuity all that it preserved, which seemed alarming in the eyes of some. Something had been sacrificed to the notion of a

6. *La vie monastique, ses principes essentiels,* trans. of Maur Wolter's *Praecipua Ordinis monastici elementa,* Maredsous, 1901, p. 142-145.

7. J. M. Besse, *Le moine bénédictin,* Liguge, 1898, p. 87.

triennial term: in fact, every three years the community should be urged to pass judgment on the government of its superior and the benefits reaped thereby; it was only after having successfully withstood this scrutiny during the course of a nine year regime that the superior, having proven himself, was definitely acknowledged as perpetual.[8]

Dom Butler treats the question with much care and at great length. His testimony is all the more important since this noted historian of monachism belonged to the English congregation and had "taken advantage of the privilege" of Leo XIII to be elected abbot of Downside first for eight years, and a second time for twelve years. He affirms that the government of a monastery by a perpetual abbot is the system of government which is consistent with the Rule of Saint Benedict.

Saint Benedict actually gives the abbot an unlimited discretionary power in all matters and charges him with an equally unlimited and undivided responsibility. His fundamental idea is that the responsibility will be the counter-balance of the power, a balance sufficient to assure a just and fitting practice. And this purely religious check is the only one that Saint Benedict provides to meet the ordinary circumstances; in the case of extraordinary occurrences, he has recourse to the intervention of the diocesan bishop. Unless very serious disorders should arise in the normal, healthy functioning of the monastery, it is this union of power and responsibility which Saint Benedict trusts as the form of government best suited to the results which he envisions in his Rule.

He adds that an abbot named for three, four or eight years cannot have a full sense of his responsibility according to the spirit of Saint Benedict, for the good reason that he is not and cannot be responsible in this way. In the system of checks and balances devised to replace this feeling of the abbot's responsibility, the power passes from the hands of the abbot, who becomes a mere official, into the hands of the definitory or central committee which, in fact, governs the whole congregation. For Dom Butler,

8. P. Delatte, osb, *Dom Gueranger, abbé de Solesmes*. Paris, 1909, I, p. 193.

the sacrifice of perpetuity likewise deals a blow at one of the most fundamental conceptions of Saint Benedict: that of the paternal authority of the abbot, in the Benedictine sense of these words.

Saint Benedict has based his theory of the life of the community on ideas springing from analogies with the natural family situation. For him, in the concept of the monastic life, the name of "father" is not merely a spiritual title: it implies a fullness and a reality, springing from the fact that the community is established and organized in imitation of the natural family. But the relationship between father and child is, by its very essence, stable; it can only be severed by death. Besides, for the formation and maintenance of a family spirit, a certain stability within the community is necessary; this is only possible with the perpetuity of the abbatial charge. Dom Butler concludes that, if the system of temporary abbots or priors has indeed produced good results in the past, it was not without a serious drawback; it has missed a principal element in the thought of Saint Benedict and, consequently, the life led in these monasteries was not a complete Benedictine life. After this, the wise abbot admits that perpetuity has its drawbacks also, but that any system of government has these, that they are not as great as the advantages and that, besides, remedies or palliatives can be found. In any case, he says:

> It is a much healthier method of legislation to provide special means for acting according to eventualities, than to legislate with the idea that the eventualities themselves will be the rule. A legislation cannot be constructed with chief deference paid to the abuses. . . . To make the exception the basis of legislation and to anticipate these contingencies by dislocating and destroying the central ideas of Saint Benedict on the government and life of his monasteries: this is to apply a remedy which is certainly worse than the illness.[9]

Dom Molitor, abbot of Saint Joseph of Gerleve in Westphalia, an expert in monastic law, declares himself likewise in favor of the

9. C. Butler, *Benedictine Monachism, op. cit.*, p. 237–244.

lifetime regime because, according to him, perpetuity is required by the nature of the paternal authority which is the basis of the system of the monastic family. He adds that the members of this family, being stable, necessarily entail the stability of their superior. On the contrary, in the modern orders established on the principle of centralization, all the religious can be transferred from one house to another, from which necessarily follows the frequent change of superiors. Besides, it is much easier to find a superior every three years in an entire province than in one single monastery. Dom Molitor also points out that there are inconveniences in having several abbots in the same house, given the fact that, after their term of office, they preserve a certain dignity and the insignia which were conferred on them at the time of their solemn benediction. The fact that the abbot is "enthroned" also constitutes an argument in support of perpetuity: actually, in the ancient law, any ecclesiastical person having a "see" is considered to be stable. By way of confirmation, Dom Molitor sums up the reasons given by the Constitutions of the Society of Jesus for establishing the perpetuity of the general. He adds that the perpetuity is in terms of the responsibilities and the extent of the superior's powers: in the modern congregations where the rules and constitutions specify all the details of the religious life, the superiors can change frequently without inconvenience, on the contrary in the monastic orders the powers of the abbot are much more extensive. He points out that perpetuity is better suited for cloistered orders than for active orders. Finally, he notes that the frequent change of superiors is natural in the orders where they are not elected by their community but appointed by a superior authority.[10]

Cardinal Schuster, former abbot of Saint Paul Outside the Walls in Rome, is no less affirmative on the subject of the appropriateness of abbatial perpetuity. He writes that the ancients found it difficult to conceive of a spiritual fatherhood which was not at the same time definitive and perpetual; this is why Canon Law has made all ecclesiastical benefices perpetual. Besides, the concept of family

10. Cf. R. Molitor, OSB, *Religiosi Juris Capita selecta,* Ratisbonne, 1909, 406–413.

under which Saint Benedict instituted the monastery requires that the father be always father. The school of service of the Lord also demands the permanence of the abbot, the representative of Christ in the supernatural formation and education of his disciples.[11]

Dom Columba Marmion, abbot of Maredsous, for his part, writes:

From this same principle of the *patria potestas* likewise flows this application: the power of the abbot, like that of the Sovereign Pontiff, is for life, that is to say that only Divine Providence terminates the exercise of his authority at the same moment that he ends his days. In other more modern institutions, the superiors called priors, guardians or rectors are elected every three years: for these institutes, it is a condition of vitality and perfection; in the monastic society, which forms one family, the abbot, called "Father," usually keeps his power for life. That is one of the characteristics of the cenobitical existence, and it cannot be modified without upsetting, by the same stroke, one of the essential principles of our institution. For the monk, this continuity of the abbot's power assures him, in greater measure, the "blessings of obedience" which he has come to seek in the cloister. Moreover, this form of government is based on that which Christ himself, Eternal Wisdom, has given to his Church.[12]

These authors have the obvious purpose, not of establishing facts according to documents nor of proving them, but of justifying an existing practice. Their arguments are not all of equal worth: some are only pertinent for a particular period and not for the primitive tradition. Nor should the analogy between spiritual fatherhood and family and natural fatherhood and family be pushed too far: it is a modern concept and is not found thus formulated in the Rule of Saint Benedict. What must be retained from these texts, without the need of approving all the arguments, is the firm conviction of all these authors that abbatial perpetuity is what best responds to the institution and organization of the monastic life.

11. Cf. I. Cardinal Schuster, *La Regula monasteriorum,* Turin, 1942, 438–440.

12. C. Marmion, OSB, *Christ, the Ideal of the Monk,* (St Louis, Mo.: B. Herder, 1964), p. 88–89.

CHAPTER TWELVE

CONCLUSION

THE LIFETIME REGIME of superiors in monastic orders is a well established institution. It has its roots in the primitive conception of the cenobitical life. If it was not originally made explicit in precise formulas, this is because it was considered to be inherent in the institution, flowing from its very nature. Soon enough, authentic texts emanating from the popes and the councils gave it the force of law, and it actually was never directly contested. No one during the whole of the High Middle Ages would have thought to make the abbatial office a temporary charge, renewable at regular intervals, fixed in advance, by successive electoral votes. When they deposed abbots, the princes, as proprietors of monasteries or as political sovereigns, and the bishops, as ecclesiastical superiors, had no other purpose than to install in their place candidates of their own choice, without considering any sort of time limit. It has been seen that the numerous documents concerning freedom of election or privileges proclaim the lifetime character of the abbatial charge by confirming that a new abbot does not succeed his predecessor until the latter's death. In the tenth century, when Cluny undertook monastic reform, it was not from opposition to perpetuity that the monasteries affiliated with the great abbey were only governed by revocable priors; this was solely to deliver all these monasteries from the control of proprietors and magnates. The conception of the Order of Cluny made these priories simple dependent houses; there was only one independent monastery, the great abbey whose abbot was chosen for life.

Perpetuity was thus juridically safeguarded in the only way that it could be under the given circumstances; the fact of Cluny proves nothing against the system of lifetime abbots. In any case, the system recovered all of its former vigor in the Order of Cîteaux whose monasteries were independent and governed by perpetual abbots. The principle was so well established and so universally admitted that new orders, Carthusians, Camaldolese, Vallombrosans, Canons Regular, and even the Mendicants, at first had perpetual major superiors. The Decree of Gratian only recognized and sanctioned this fact. Even when the decadence of the fourteenth century and the commendam brought about well-known abuses, perpetuity itself was not attacked, and never completely disappeared, especially in the Germanic countries. The commendatory abbots themselves, and with reason, held fast to the notion that they were perpetual. When the monastic life was re-established with its different forms in all countries after the disasters at the end of the eighteenth century, there was a gradual return to the lifetime abbatial charge in spite of certain difficulties due to ignorance of the genuine tradition.

And yet, in the course of this history, the institution suffered numerous transformations. There is hardly any fairly long period when it did not meet with serious difficulties. Beginning in the Merovingian Period, seculars intervene in the life of the abbeys and in abbatial nominations and bishops interpret their right of surveillance over the monasteries in a very broad and authoritative manner. But it was mainly during the Carolingian Period that the principle of lifetime abbots was most disregarded, at least in many countries. The kings laid hands on the abbeys and the abbatial office. Most of the abbots, having become the "faithful" of the prince, only retained their charge as long as they were politically useful. Then with the weakening of Carolingian political structure, the monasteries fell under the *dominatio* of territorial chiefs. These were more jealous of a less legitimate and less assured power exercised on a lower scale than that of the king. The monasteries became the stakes in the struggles among these chiefs.

To these difficulties were added other more profound ones. Many abbots allowed themselves to be carried away, leading a very external and worldly life, playing the part of lords and abandoning their essential religious role of father and physician of their monks. Some even went so far as to forget their monastic vocation. It is against these deformities that Benedict of Aniane first attempted a reform. At the same time, a certain number of monks reacted by leaving their monasteries to devote themselves in solitude to the ascetical life and to prayer. The Cluniac reform went to the root of the evil by wresting the monastic order from the spirit of the world as well as from the control of seculars. But to do this, it was led to suppress the abbots in its dependent monasteries. The lifetime principle is concentrated in one abbey which heads the Order. Cîteaux re-established abbatial perpetuity and sought to provide a counter-balance to remedy the dangers which it implied. Nevertheless, a century later, the spirit of the world again usurped the abbatial charge. The organization of regular visitations and of general chapters became more necessary. Soon, however, this was no longer sufficient. In the new orders and in the young monastic congregations, this led, then, to the consideration of a temporary regime for superiors, at first under a rather flexible form, as among the Carthusians, the Carmelites and the Servites; then in a more rigid manner, by fixing once for all, for each category of superiors, the term of their office, which was usually a three or four year period, sometimes less. The decadence of the fourteenth century and the extension of the commendam system only served to generalize this regime. The monastic congregations from the fifteenth to the seventeenth century nearly all adopted the rule of temporary superiors. So much so that, before the great restoration of the nineteenth century, abbatial perpetuity had been all but forgotten, although it still subsisted in some countries and in some orders.

All of these obstacles to perpetuity are not equally opposed to the institution: some are external, whereas others spring from dangers inherent in the system itself. The control of seculars and princes over the abbeys, the interferences of bishops in the monastic life, the excessive interventions of the ·Roman Curia, and the commendam constitute the purely extrinsic causes; they have nothing to do with the lifetime regime, and they could have occurred with temporary abbots. Ambition, a worldly spirit, bad administration, the enticement of wealth, and misconduct, on the contrary, are dangers inherent in a situation which is stable and of long duration when the personal consciousness of religious responsibility is no longer sufficiently alive and when there is lacking either adequate means of surveillance and control or a supreme authority capable of intervening in case of necessity. Other inconveniences result from age and illness. They can render a superior incapable of fulfilling his function for the common good, both spiritual and temporal. It is therefore important to find, amid historical facts, the elements which, without being opposed to perpetuity, allow for the perfecting of the primitive institution by assuring the reasonable guaranties of a good government in the form desired by the founders.

The remedies employed at Cluny, Saint Justine, Valladolid and Saint Maur responded to exceptional situations of unprecedented gravity, but they actually resulted from external dangers. On the contrary, the grouping of abbeys into federations, even their union in congregations, with a supreme authority, the regular and frequent meetings of the general chapters and the organized canonical visitations, without touching the institution of lifetime abbots have proven their effectiveness for remedying the dangers inherent in perpetuity. The Church has well understood this, since it has made these palliatives obligatory for all religious orders, even those which have only temporary abbots.

The history which has just been retraced does not present itself as the evolution of an institution trying to find its definitive form. The lifetime abbatial regime is not a primitive expression which developed, becoming more precise and more perfect, ending in a temporary regime as in its final perfection. On the contrary, perpetuity appears in the monastic life as an essential element which has always subsisted, at least in some areas, which has stood its ground when it did not encounter external obstacles, and which reappears when these latter eventually disappear. The tendency has always been to preserve or attempt to recover stability in the

L

government of abbeys. It is not by chance that the new flowering of
the monastic orders during the nineteenth and twentieth centuries,
comparable to the ages of the past, coincides with a general recovery
of the lifetime abbatial regime. The return to sources, the restoration of monastic life in conformity with the best traditions and, at
the same time, wisely adapted to the conditions of modern life,
has led restorers of the various orders or congregations to re-
establish the lifetime abbatial charge. This is all the more remarkable
since it is not a question of an undertaking that is limited in time or
space. The restorations have been numerous, extending over more
than a century and to all continents. They have been accomplished
with a certain spirit, with extremely diverse preoccupations and
aims in view, and yet all, save for a few exceptions, call for the
perpetuity of abbots. It remains to be seen whether the means of
controlling the government of the abbots—general chapters and
visitations—as they are used today, are still sufficiently efficacious,
or whether they should be perfected.

   On the one hand, the abbot is elected by his community after the
death of the predecessor. Saint Gregory's text keeps its full force:
"*neque viventi abbate quaecumque persona qualibet occasione in suo
monasterio praeponatur.*" The ancient law has never been abrogated:
"*Defuncto abbate cuiusquam congregationis non extraneus eligatur. . . .*"
Once installed, the abbot contracts a bond with his abbey that can
only be annulled by the superior authority (that is the Holy See
for the monasteries which are now exempt). But, on the other hand,
each abbey is no longer in the same position as it was during the
High Middle Ages. It is no longer isolated from others, to be
simply under the surveillance of a bishop who extended his jurisdiction over all the religious establishments of his diocese. Today, as a
rule, the abbeys are united among themselves into congregations
whose extension more or less coincides with that of a given nation.
Exempt, they depend on a remote authority, that of the Holy See.
Monastic congregations are defined by Canon Law: "*Plurium
monasterium sui iuris inter se coniunctio sub eodem superiore,*" which
includes two elements: a real union among the monasteries and
submission to a superior. Since the entity of this union and the

authority of this superior are not specified, it belongs to the constitutions of each group to specify them; subject to the approbation of the Holy See, to give them force of law. It is the way in which each congregation realizes what constitutes its own proper physiognomy and makes it a distinct *religio*, a subject of law similar to an order properly so called. Nevertheless, it is evident that this union and this submission to a superior also determine and limit the autonomy and the fact of being *sui iuris*. The monasteries united into congregations are autonomous to the extent and according to the limits foreseen by the constitutions. These are the particular law for each one of them, and all must recognize the same authority, take part in general chapters, and submit to the anticipated canonical visitations. Submission to a superior authority, common usages, and control of the observance and administration according to the proper statutes of each congregation, constitute, for the abbey of today, a particular law which, while it safeguards a certain autonomy, is no longer the independence of former times. These same conditions determine the exercise of the abbatial function; the abbot is a major superior, but according to the conditions and limits fixed by the constitutions. According to the measure of these conditions, he is responsible to the authority of the congregation; he must submit, in all that is established by the constitutions, to the supreme authority. Consequently, this latter has the duty, in the person of the visitators, the president or the superior general, the definitory or the general chapter, to intervene in case of difficulty, weakness, inadequacy or incompetence of the abbot, to safeguard the common good of the community and of the congregation, within the limits of the particular law established by the constitutions. The authority of the congregation, in whatever person or college it resides, is thus the counter-balance of abbatial perpetuity.

To promote the exercise of this power and facilitate the interventions of this authority, while taking into account the lessons of history and the experiences of the past, and in order to avoid the question of persons, would it not be wise to anticipate the methods according to which the principle of perpetuity would be applied in each monastic order and congregation? It appears clear enough that certain dangers or difficulties could be avoided if there existed sufficiently precise prescriptions concerning the duration of the government of abbots, especially when questions of age and illness intervene. An increase in the number of members of the supreme authority of the congregation could be very useful in helping to make the necessary decisions. But rather than impose a uniform regulation, would it not be prudent for each order or congregation to set down in its constitutions whatever the general chapter deems most useful? It would be very harmful to the monastic state to seriously attack the lifetime regime: this would be touching on one of its essential elements.

In the government of monasteries, as in other human affairs, abuses will never be completely avoided, nor will all the difficulties and failures ever be suppressed; but prudence requires that the necessary precautions be taken, all the more so when it is a question of the good of souls and the proper administration of Church goods. It is not because Saint Benedict or the other founders did not foresee all these things, or because monastic life is not developing today under the same conditions as in their time, that we must hold fast to a primitive legislation and a situation which lacks precision. Formerly, the proximity of the bishop, whose authority was effective over all the monasteries, could render any other intervention superfluous. Later on, with the exemption and the grouping of abbeys across all of Christendom, the Cistercians were attentive to the need of establishing means of control and a supreme authority, by means of canonical visitations, the system of filiations and the general chapter. This institution has proven itself: it is enough to make it more precise and more perfect.

Beyond institutions and law, it is to the spirit that created them that we must always return. The perpetuity of the abbot was born of the idea of spiritual fatherhood. To the extent that the abbot fulfills this paternal role, he preserves something of the traditional figure of the abbot. This explains the success of Cluny and the monastic reforms of the sixteenth and seventeenth centuries, in spite of passing and accidental failures of the lifetime principle. It is not the notion of spiritual fatherhood that has assured the duration of the lifetime abbatial charge through the centuries, but the latter has been the more authentic and fruitful as it has drawn closer to this ideal.

The profound justification for the perpetuity of the abbot is the stability of the monk. Devoted to the quest of "the city whose foundations are eternal" (Epistle to the Hebrews), he leads a life separated and detached from the world, the better to belong to the One to whom he has given himself. He has entered into a permanent regime which does not merely consist in purely spiritual exercises, but which is made up of a material framework and a code of external observances by means of which he actualizes his belonging to Christ. Now one of the aspects of this code of observance is stability in the same human milieu, and not only in the same spiritual quest.[1] If the same community of brothers is called to seek Christ by the practice of mutual charity, it is logical and natural that the one who directs and guides them in this quest for God should also be stable. The Rule of Saint Benedict suggests this sufficiently by proclaiming this leader to be the representative of Christ and by giving him the name of *Abba, Pater*.[2]

1. "Officina vero ubi haec omnia (instrumenta bonorum operum) diligenter operemur claustra sunt monasterii et stabilitas in congregatione." RB 4:78.

2. "Abbas . . . Christi enim vices in monasterio creditur, quando ipsius vocatur pro nomine, dicente Apostolo: Accepistis spiritum adoptionis filiorum, in quo clamamus: abba, pater." RB 2:2f.

BIBLIOGRAPHY

Albers, B., *Conseutudines Monasticae*. Monte Cassino, 1907.

Baucher, J., Art. *Abbé*, in *Dictionnaire de Droit Canon*. Paris, 1935.

Berlière, U., *L'Ordre monastique des origines au XIIe siècle*, in Collection "Pax," 29 éd. Paris, 1921.

——*Les élections abbatiales au moyen âge*, in Académie royale de Belgique. Lettres. Mémoires. in-8°2 Séries, t. XX, fasc. 3. Brussels, 1927.

Besse, J. M., *Les moines d'Orient antérieurs au concile de Chalcédoine* (451). Paris, 1900.

——*Les moines de l'ancienne France*, Archives de la France monastique, v. 2, Paris, 1906.

Bibliotheca cluniacensis, in qua S. S. Patrum Abbatum Cluniacensium vitae, miracula, scripta, statuta, privilegia, chronologiaque duplex . . . collegerunt D. M. Marrier et A. Quercetanus. Macon, 1915.

Butler, C., *Benedictine Monachism*. 2 ed. New York, 1924.

Canivez, J. M., *Statuta Capitulorum generalium Ordinis Cisterciensis ab anno 1116 ad annum 1786*, 8 vol. Louvain, 1933 sq.

Congar, Y. *"Quod omnes tangit,"* in *Revue historique du Droit*, 1958, p. 210 ff.

Congregationis S. Justinae de Padua O. S. B. ordinationes capitulorum generalium, ed. Leccisotti, Monte Cassino, 1939.

Corpus juris canonici, ed. Friedberg, 2 vol. Leipzig, 1879–1881.

Dereine, Ch., Art. *Chanoines*, in *Dictionnaire d'Histoire et de Géographie ecclésiatique*, 1953.

Duerr, L., *Heilige Vaterschaft im antieken Orient*, in *Heilige Ueberlieferung. Festgabe . . . J. Herwegen*, Munster en W., 1938, p. 1–20.

Edmonds, H., Art. *Abt*, in *Reallexion für Antinke und Christentum*, I, 45–55.

Ewald-Hartmann, *Epistolae*, in *Monumenta Germaniae Historica*, 4°, 1887–1899.

Gaudemet, J., *L'Eglise dans l'Empire romain*, Paris, 1958.

Gougaud, L., *Ermites et Reclus. Etudes sur d'anciennes formes de vie religieuse*, Ligugé, 1928.

Gratiani Decretum, . . .Gregorii XIII ed. Venice, 1591.

Gratien, P., *Histoire de la fondation et de l'évolution de l'Ordre des Frères Min eurs au XIIIe siècle*. Paris, 1928.

Hardouin, J., *Acta Conciliorum.* 11 vol. Paris, 1715.

Hausherr, I., *La direction spirituelle en Orient autrefois,* in *Orientalia Christiana Analecta,* 144. Rome, 1955.

Hefele-Leclercq, *Histoire des Conciles.* trad. française. 20 vol. Paris, 1907 sq.

Holzapfel, H., *Manuale Historiae Ordinis Fratum Minorum,* trans. Hasebbek. Freiburgi Br., 1909.

Hourlier. J., *Le chapitre général jusqu'au moment du Grand Schisme. Origine, développement.* Paris, 1936.

Jaffe-Wattenbach, *Regesta pontificum romanorum.* 2 vol., Berlin, 1885–1888.

Krusch-Levison, *Passiones vitaeque sanctorum aevi merovingici. Monumenta Germaniae Historica,* Scrip. rer. meroving., t. II-VII, 1896–1920.

Ladeuze, P., *Etude sur le cénobitisme pakomien pendant le IVe siècle et la première moitié du Ve.* Louvain, 1898.

Lemarigner, J. F., *Structures monastiques et structures politiques dans la France de la fin du Xe et des débuts du XIe siècle,* in *Il monachesimo nell' alto mediovo e la formazione della civillà occidentale. Settimana di studio del centro italiano di studi sull'alto medioevo,* IV, Spoleto, 1957, p. 382–400.

Lesne, E., *Histoire de la propriété ecclésiastique en France,* 6 vol. Paris, 1910–1943.

Levy-Bruhl, H., *Etude sur les élections abbatiales en France, I. Période franque.* Paris, 1913.

Maassen, F., *Concilia aevi merovingici, Monumenta Germaniae Historica,* 4°, Scrip. rer. meroving, Concilia I, 1893.

Mabillon, J., *Acta sanctorum O. S. B.,* 9 vol., Paris 1668–1702 (rééd. Solesmes, 1935.

——*Annales Ordines S. Benedicti,* 5 tomes. Lucques, 1739.

McLaughlin, Th. P., *Le très ancien droit monastique de l'Occident,* in *Archives de la France monastique,* XXXVIII. Ligugé, 1935.

Mahn, J. B., *L'Ordre cistercien et son gouvernement des origines au milieu du XIIIe siècle* (Bibliothèque des Ecoles Françaises d'Athènes et de Rome, 161), Paris, 1945.

Martène, E., *Histoire de la Congrégation de Saint-Maur,* éd. Charvin (Archives de la France monastique), 10 vol. Ligugé, 1928–1943.

Meester (de) P., *De monachico statu iuxta disciplinam byzantinam, Statuta selectis fontibus et commentariis instructa* (S. Congregazione per la Chiesa Orientale. Codificazione canonica orientale. Fonti. ser. II, fasc. X). Rome, 1942.

Menologium cisterciense a monachis Ordinis Cisterciensis Strictioris Observantiae compositium. Westmalle, 1952.

Moulin, L., *Le gouve.nement des communautés religieuses comme type de gouvernement mixte,* in *Revue française de science politique,* 1952, 335–355.

——*La science politique et le gouvernement des communautés religieuses,* in *Revue internationale des sciences administratives,* 1951, p. 42–67.

——*Les origines religieuses des techniques électorales et délibératives modernes,* in *Revue internationale d'Histoire politique et constitutionnelle,* 1953.

——*Il governo degli ordini religiosi,* in *Studi politici,* 2, 1953–1954.

——*"Sanior et maior pars,"* in *Revue historique du droit,* 1958, 368ff.

Noschitzka, C. L., *Die kirchenrechtliche Stellung des resignierten Regularabtes unter besonderer Brucksichtigung der Geschichtlichen Entwickling im Zisterzienserorden.* Rome, 1957

Oliger, R., *Les évêques réguliers. Recherche sur leur condition juridique depuis les origines du monachisme jusqu'à la fin du moyen âge* (Museum Lessianum). Paris, 1958.

Pantin, W. A., *Documents Illustrating the Activities of the General and Provincial Chapters of the English Black Monks,* 1215-1540, in *The royal historical Society,* XLV, XLVII, LIV. London, 1931–1937.

Penco. G., *Storia del monachesimo in Italia, Tempi e Figure* 31. Rome, 1960.

Perez de Urbel, J., *Les monjes espanoles en la edad media,*2 vol. Madrid, 2 ed., s.d.

de Puniet. J., Art. *Abbé,* in *Dictionnaire de spiritualité,* I, 49–57.

Schmitz. Ph., *Histoire de l'Ordre de saint Benoit,* 7 vol. Maredsous, 1942–1956.

Schnuerer. G., *L'Eglise et la civilisation au moyen âge,* trans. Castella, 3 vol. Paris, 1933–1948.

Schneider, Art. *Abbas,* in *Mittellateinisches Wörterbuch bis zum ausgehenden* 13 *Jahrhundert,* I, 8–10.

Tamburinius, *De Jure Abbatum et aliorum praelatorum, tam regularium quam saecularium, episcopis inferiorum.* 3 vol. Lyon, 1650.

Tassi, Ild., *Ludovico Barbo* (1381–1443) (Uomini e dottrine, I) Rome, 1952.

Thomassin, *Ancienne et nouvelle discipline de l'Eglise touchant les bénéfices et les bénéficiers.* 3 vol. Paris, 1725.

Turk, J., *Charta caritatis prior,* in *Analecta S. Ordinis Cisterciensis* I, 1945, 11–61.

Turk, J., *Cistercii Statuta antiquissima. Instituta generalia capituli apud Cistercium, Exordium Cisterciensis coenobii, Charta caritatis,* in *Analecta S. Ord. Cisterciensis* IV, 1948, 1–159.

de Valous, G., *Le monachisme clunisien des origines au XVᵉ siècle. Vie intérieure des monastères et organisation de l'Ordre.* 2 vol. Ligugé, 1935.

Volk, P., *Die Generalkapitels-Rezesse der Bursfelder Kongregation,* 3 vol. Siegburg, 1955–1959.

Werminghoff, A., *Concilia aevi karolini, Monumenta Germaniae Historica,* Legum sectio III, 3 vol., 1906 sq.

Zeumer, K., *Formulae merovingici et karolini aevi. Monumenta Germaniae Historica,* Legum sectio V, 1886.

Zimmermann, A. M., *Kalendarium Benedictinum,* 3 vol. Metten, 1933–1937.

INDEX OF PROPER NAMES

The following abbreviations are used: ab = abbey, abp = archbishop, abt = abbot, bp = bishop, c = cardinal, cgr = congregation, ct = count, e = emperor, f = founder, k = king, n = note, p = pope, pr = prior, pry = priory, q = queen.

Laus tibi Christi